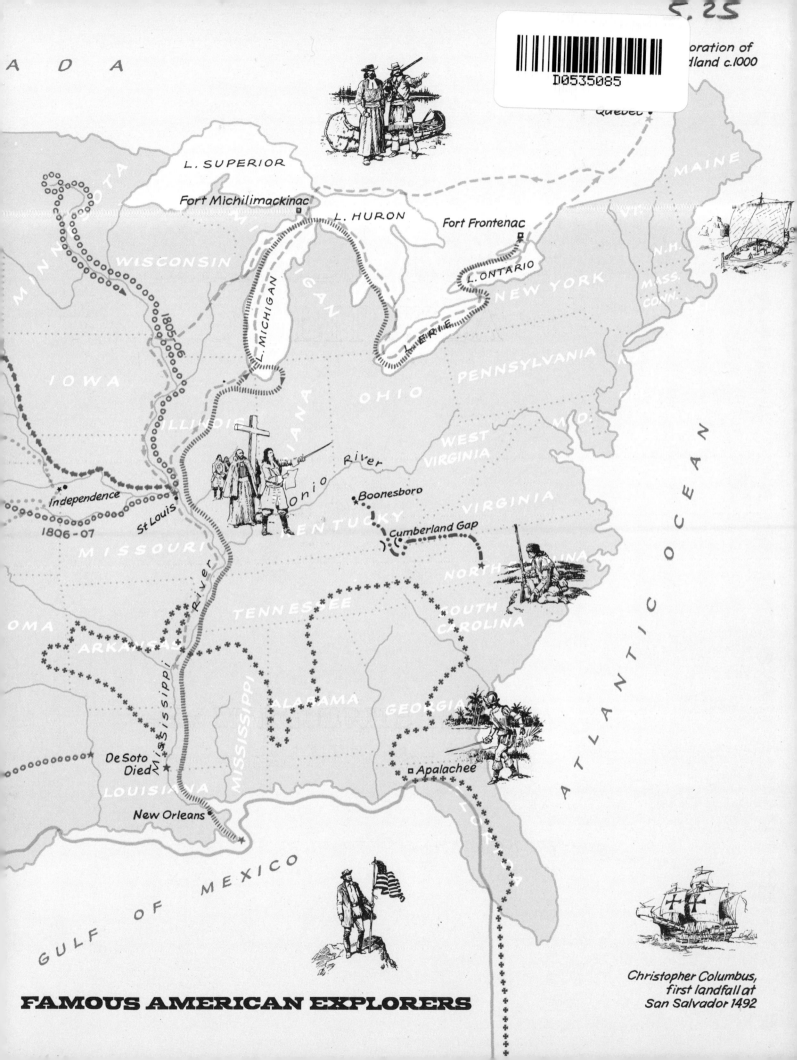

FAMOUS AMERICAN EXPLORERS

*...oration of
...dland c.1000*

D0535085

*Christopher Columbus,
first landfall at
San Salvador 1492*

Place labels:

L. SUPERIOR
Fort Michilimackinac
L. HURON
Fort Frontenac
L. ONTARIO
L. ERIE
Quebec
MAINE
N.H.
MASS.
CONN.
NEW YORK
PENNSYLVANIA
MINNESOTA
WISCONSIN
MICHIGAN
L. MICHIGAN
IOWA
ILLINOIS
INDIANA
OHIO
WEST VIRGINIA
MD.
VIRGINIA
1805-06
Independence
1806-07
St. Louis
MISSOURI
Ohio River
Boonesboro
KENTUCKY
Cumberland Gap
NORTH CAROLINA
SOUTH CAROLINA
TENNESSEE
ARKANSAS
Mississippi River
De Soto Died
ALABAMA
MISSISSIPPI
GEORGIA
Apalachee
LOUISIANA
New Orleans
OMA
OKLAHOMA
GULF OF MEXICO
ATLANTIC OCEAN
ADA
CANADA

Famous American Explorers

Famous American Explorers

By BERN KEATING

Line Drawings by LORENCE BJORKLUND

RAND MCNALLY & COMPANY · CHICAGO · NEW YORK · SAN FRANCISCO

Library of Congress Cataloging in Publication Data

Keating, Bern.
FAMOUS AMERICAN EXPLORERS.

SUMMARY: Traces the journeys and adventures of
those who explored the North American continent in-
cluding the Spanish conquistadores, the Vikings, French
Voyageurs, and mountain men.
1. America—Discovery and exploration—Juvenile
literature. [1. America—Discovery and exploration. 2.
Explorers] I. Bjorklund, Lorence F., illus. II. Title.
E101.K4 917.3'04 72-4079
ISBN 0-528-82480-5
ISBN 0-528-82481-3 (lib. ed.)

Printed in the United States of America
by RAND MCNALLY & COMPANY

First printing, 1972
Second printing, 1974

FRONT COVER:
*Alexander Mackenzie at
the Mouth of the Bella Coola River*
By Frederic Remington
COLLECTION OF DR. HAROLD MC CRACKEN

Contents

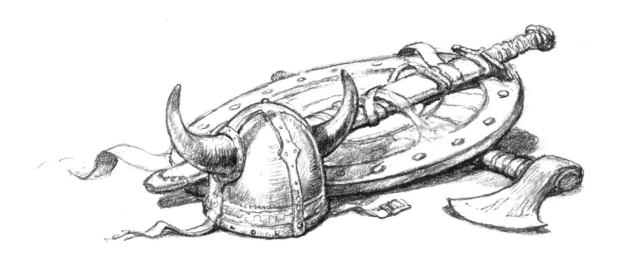

Five Centuries Before Columbus

SEATED AMONG HIS VIKING COMRADES in their banquet hall, his face dimly lighted by a flickering fire in the cooking pit, Bjarni Herjolfsson held the Norse settlers of Greenland fascinated with his story of being swallowed by a fog and carried by currents far west of where any European sailor had ever been before.

All Vikings were sailors at heart, no matter how many cows they milked on their northern farms, so the Greenlanders followed Bjarni's story with keen professional interest. They nodded approval when he told how he had known, after the fog lifted, that the land to westward was not Greenland, because it had no mountains capped with glaciers near the shore. They understood how he had known he was too far south by the elevation of the North Star. They considered it good seamanship to sail north till the North Star was at the right height and then to turn east so that he made his landfall in Greenland exactly at his father's frontier farm.

Bjarni's story stirred the adventurous spirit of those pioneers on the farthest outpost of the Viking world. But the hard demands of their farmlands, newly carved out of the grim subarctic wilderness of Greenland's western coast, kept them prisoners ashore. All but one, a young boy who sat outside the circle of grown men and devoured each detail of Bjarni's adventure.

Leif, the son of Eric the Red who was founder and chief of the Greenland Norse colony, swore that when he was old enough to command a Viking ship and crew, he would sail westward to found a new Viking colony just as his father had done a few years before by sailing from Iceland to then-unknown Greenland.

Leif's first voyage as a Viking sea captain was to the Norse mother country in Norway, where Leif became a Christian before returning to his Greenland home. The date is easy to remember. It was probably the year 1000.

Shortly after returning to his home in Greenland, Leif loaded a boat with supplies and enlisted a 35-man crew for an exploratory trip to find the strange land Bjarni had described years before. He was even in the same boat, for he had bought it from Bjarni, who never went to sea again after he was criticized by some Vikings for not being curious enough to go ashore in the New World he had discovered.

Leif's new boat was not the dragon-headed warship used by Vikings to raid civilized European coasts. It was a *knarr*, a fat-bellied craft built for carrying bigger loads and riding heavier seas than the rakish war *drakars*. Rigged with a single square sail, the *knarr* spared the crew the hard job of rowing whenever the wind was fair.

Sailing west, the Norsemen raised land, just as Bjarni had said they would. Unlike the timid Bjarni, Leif went ashore and thus became the first European that we know of to put foot to soil in the New World. It was probably the year 1001, almost 500 years before Columbus went ashore far to the south.

Leif found no grass in that grim land and little useful timber. From the shore to the great glaciers looming far to the west, the land was a desolate, flat rock. Leif made a statement that is mildly scornful of the Viking who had been there before him.

"We have not failed to land like Bjarni. Now I will call this country *Helluland*—the Land of Flat Stone."

He turned his back on Helluland, for Viking colonists had to have good pasturage for their cattle and timber to build boats. We know now that Helluland is almost certainly Baffin Island. Anybody who has ever seen Baffin Island from the sea has to agree that Leif was wise in pressing on southward, for it is a grim, frozen waste.

A few days' sail to the south he came to the first spot we can pinpoint exactly. Leif was struck by the beauty of wide sandy beaches curving up from the sea. On that rocky coast, only one spot—a 35-mile stretch of Labrador's shoreline—has a sandy beach. More wonderful to Leif than the sand, however, was the magnificent stand of black spruce trees, sorely needed back in Greenland where no forests grew.

"This land shall be named for its riches," Leif said. "It shall be called *Markland*—Land of Forests."

Sailing southward, they made a landfall in a cove with a meadow stretching back from the beach. The rivers were full of salmon and the meadow full of berries. So they decided to winter there. They built huts and brought ashore their sheepskin sleeping bags. When the weather permitted, they split into two parties to explore the new land.

Leif thought the country ideal for a Viking settlement. In the spring he sailed for home, carrying a load of timber. The old saga that tells Leif's story also reports his *knarr* was loaded down with grapes that grew wild. Those grapes have vexed historians for centuries.

The name he gave his colony was *Vinland*, which many historians have interpreted to mean Land of Vines because of the grapes. No vines grow farther north than Massachusetts, so historians have tried to plant Leif's Vinland everywhere along the Atlantic seashore as far south as Florida.

The truth is far more likely that the grapes were added to Leif's true story centuries after his death. *Vinland* in Old Norse means Land of Meadows. And Leif picked his campsite in Vinland precisely because a meadow stretched back from a sheltered cove.

The argument of where Vinland is just about ended in 1961 when a Norwegian historian, cleverly following clues given in the poetic saga about Leif's voyages, began digging at the far northern tip of Newfoundland and turned up the site of a Norse settlement dated at about 1000. Curiously, the place-name today, almost a thousand years after Leif's day, is still a fair translation for Vinland. It is L'Anse aux Meadows, or Meadow Cove.

The Greenlanders made three efforts to settle in Newfoundland at Leif's village. They had a blacksmith shop, cattle, boathouses, all the buildings and equipment needed by Norsemen to survive.

But they made one stupid mistake. An exploring party wantonly killed eight natives they found sleeping under canoes. The Vikings called them *Skrellings*, a word with several meanings, all of them insulting. We do not know if they were Indians or Eskimos, for both people used that

13

OVERLEAF: *The Landing of Leif Ericson in the New World in 1001* A.D. By Edward Moran
COURTESY, U.S. NAVAL ACADEMY MUSEUM

*The Debarkation of Columbus,
Morning of October 12, 1492*
By Edward Moran
COURTESY, U.S. NAVAL ACADEMY MUSEUM

own worries, he realized he could not handle three ships in mutiny by himself. Betting everything on those fresh leaves and berries, he asked his captains to give him three days more sailing westward. He promised he would turn back if land was still not in sight.

As the days ran out, the good signs multiplied, but the men were stubborn, and Columbus knew he was racing against time. He rarely left the deck.

Midnight passed, beginning the last day before he would have to abandon his search for a short sea route to China by sailing west from Europe instead of traveling east over thousands of miles of dusty and dangerous camel-caravan roads.

The wind quickened again, rising to dangerous strength, but Columbus pressed on more sail. Throwing spray far to the sides, the *Santa Maria* labored through heavy seas. The sailors were drenched, but the captain had offered a prize to the first hand who sighted land, so almost everybody stayed awake, peering forward in the hope of winning the reward.

Always a faster sailor than the other two ships, the *Niña* and the *Santa Maria*, the square-rigged *Pinta* ran away from the others. At two in the morning of October 12, 1492, a sailor named Rodrigo de Triana aboard the *Pinta* entered history by singing out.

"Land! . . . Land!"

Rodrigo had become the first European to see the New World since the last Norsemen sailed back to Greenland from Newfoundland almost 500 years before.

Shortening sail, the flotilla stood off shore till dawn, then sailed to the western side of the island where Columbus found a suitable harbor for anchoring and going ashore.

Columbus and his captains landed in three boats, banners flying. They knelt on the white sand and gave prayers of thanksgiving for a safe landfall. Columbus named the island San Salvador. When a few natives came out of the forest timidly offering gifts, Columbus named them Indians, for he thought he was in the Indies, halfway around the world from San Salvador.

Columbus had made the most important exploration voyage of history, had made the greatest geographical discovery of all time . . . and he did not even know it. He probably never did know it, though he returned to the New World for three more voyages. To the end of his life

he believed he had found a short route to Asia. He never knew he had made his landfall, not in the fabled Indies, but at an insignificant island in the Bahamas, a tiny outpost of a New World so vast that today, over 450 years later, large tracts remain unexplored.

Other master mariners were not so uninformed. In Bristol, a west coast English port that was home to some of the boldest sailors in Europe, a navigator from Columbus's home city of Genoa had persuaded a group of merchants to send him west in a search for a sea route to the Indies. This John Cabot touched the North American continent somewhere around Labrador, Newfoundland, or Nova Scotia in 1497. Cabot was a better geographer than Columbus and knew instantly that he had not reached China; he knew he had found a New World.

(Till recently, many histories have been full of nonsense about the ignorance in Europe of the world's shape. Columbus did not "prove" the world was spherical, and he was a long way from being the first man to have the idea. All educated men of Europe had known for almost 2,000 years the earth was a sphere. Columbus had miscalculated the circumference of the earth and thought he had reached Asia. Cabot had figured a more nearly correct circumference of the earth and knew China lay thousands of miles farther west.)

From Cabot's day onward for decades, virtually no exploration took place on the mainland of North America. Far from recognizing the New World as a vast treasure-house, European mariners saw it as a gigantic annoyance, a useless lump lying inconveniently across the path of ships trying to reach the ports of Asia.

A roll call of the great sea rovers who charted the Atlantic shores—Amerigo Vespucci, Giovanni da Verrazano, Jacques Cartier, Henry Hudson—shows that every one of them was looking for a gate through the wall of the New World, a sea route that came to be called the Northwest Passage. Over the centuries, that elusive waterway around or through the New World landmass lured hundreds of bold sailors to ruin and death, but few of them cared about the exploration of the landmass discovered by Columbus. Far from it. They were looking for a way to get around it.

True exploration of the North American landmass began in Florida 36 years after that morning when Columbus won his bet with only hours to spare.

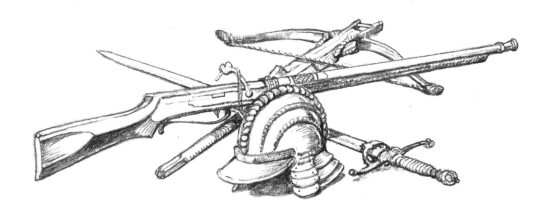

Conquistadors Seeking Gold

SITTING AROUND A CAMPFIRE in an abandoned Indian village somewhere in central Florida, several hundred armed and armored Spaniards held a war council. They had landed in 1528 on the west coast of the newly discovered land of Florida—widely believed to be an island—and had captured an Indian who told them the gold they were looking for lay far to the north at a place called Apalachee. The Spanish leader, a one-eyed, nobly-born gangster named Pánfilo de Narváez, proposed leaving the ships of their fleet and marching overland in search of Apalachee.

Pánfilo de Narváez had been in on the plunder of Mexico just a few years before—in fact he had lost his eye when he tried to hijack the loot of Cortez and was soundly trounced. Cortez had skimmed off most of the quick profits from Mexico, and so Pánfilo de Narváez had come to the "island" of Florida, hoping to find another rich empire like the Aztec, ripe for looting. Instead he had found a ferociously warlike tribe of Indians six-feet tall and capable of pulling a bow as thick as his wrist.

One of the captured Indians had given a demonstration of his strength by shooting an arrow clean through two suits of Spanish armor.

The only voice raised against the plan of marching instead of riding ships was from a battle-scarred veteran of wars in Spain and Italy, Alvar

Núñez Cabeza de Vaca, who was with the expedition as a watchdog to protect the Spanish king's split of whatever treasures they found. Cabeza de Vaca warned that the land was too swampy and the Indians too warlike to attempt a march across their country. He wanted to go to Apalachee by sea, where the Indians would have no chance to ambush them from a palmetto hammock. But Pánfilo and the other conquistadors disagreed. They were *caballeros*—that is, "horsemen," and they distrusted ships. They felt more at home even in the weird moss-hung swamps of Florida than they did at sea.

"I am guardian of the king's interest," said Cabeza de Vaca. "If you pursue this madness, I want a document saying I opposed it."

"You may have the document," said Pánfilo. "And since you are clearly frightened and unfit to travel with brave men, go in safety and take refuge in your ships."

Cabeza de Vaca leaped to his feet and drew his sword. In those days, you did not call a Spanish *hidalgo* a coward without being prepared to fight.

Cooler heads prevented the brawl, but Cabeza de Vaca then made a fateful statement.

"I refuse to go to the ships. Because I know this band is doomed and have said so publicly, it would dishonor me to leave you. I must die with you or the world will think I am a coward."

So they struck off northward together, foot soldiers and cavalry, pikemen and crossbowmen. The road was exhausting, mosquitoes swarmed, the men sickened. Indians harried the column, firing arrows from ambush and pouncing on stragglers.

Worst of all, when the Spanish reached Apalachee, they found it was a miserable village of 40 thatched huts with no hope of riches to be stolen.

They were near the present Florida-Georgia state line north of the Big Bend where Florida's Gulf Coast turns sharply westward. Hunger had set in so sharply they had forgotten about gold. When they heard of a village on the Gulf Coast where they could hope to steal a hoard of corn, they fought their way southward through constant Indian attacks.

The fleet that was to meet them failed to appear. So the Spanish *hidalgos*, who ordinarily considered work with the hands worthy only of slaves, pitched in without shame to build a fleet for escape. They threw together a rude forge and melted down spurs and armor to make saws and hammers. They killed their horses for food and made water bottles of the skins. They cut down trees and sawed out planks which they whacked together into five 33-foot boats. Sails they made from their shirts.

Half-naked and exposed to the blistering sun, starving, fever-ridden, 247 conquistadors put to sea in their ramshackle navy and turned westward, hoping to reach the Spanish settlements in Mexico. So crude was knowledge of North America at the time that Pánfilo expected to find a settlement around the next bend; it was really 1,800 miles away.

As the Spanish passed Mobile Bay, a band of Indians on the shore made friendly gestures inviting them to land. The Indians gave a feast. At the height of the festival, the Indian hosts pounced on their guests to kill and rob them. But they had made a serious tactical mistake.

Hidden in a canebrake beside the path, an Indian could perhaps bushwhack a Spaniard. But in a hand-to-hand battle the conquistador was the best fighter of the day. The soldiers carved their way to safety, leaving the ground strewn with large pieces of Indians.

Farther along, parched with thirst, they came across a large stream of muddy, fresh water far to sea—out of sight of land—the tremendous outpouring of the Mississippi River. But they sailed on westward toward what they hoped was Spanish Mexico.

During a storm, the boats were scattered. We know nothing of the fate of the other boats—probably they all capsized and the conquistadors drowned during that terrible night. But the boat under command of Cabeza de Vaca foundered on the shore of an island. We are not sure, but the landing was either at Galveston Island in Texas or Matagorda Island just south.

About 80 Spaniards washed up on the beach alive. The Indians took them in and tried to feed them. But it was bad luck that the Spanish had fallen amongst a tribe so primitive that they assumed they would lose a certain percentage of their people to starvation every winter. That poverty is hard to understand, for even today when game must be much less abundant than in those days, the seas and bays swarm with fish and oysters, and during the winter the lagoons are covered with almost solid rafts of geese and ducks. But apparently the conquistadors were no better at hunting and fishing, for they starved by the dozens, though the Indians generously gave them a share of even their starvation rations.

When only four of them remained alive, Cabeza de Vaca planned an

OVERLEAF:
The Expedition of Francisco Coronado
By Frederic Remington
COLLECTION OF DR. HAROLD MC CRACKEN

escape. The others agreed. During the great orgy of eating on the plains near present-day Alice, Texas, when the prickly pear fruits ripened, the four men simply walked off to the west and out of sight. They had been living with the Texas Indians for six years.

One of the four, incidentally, was Estebanico, the first black man to put foot in North America. One of Columbus's pilots had been called *il negro*—"the black man." But he had not come ashore in North America, indeed had never seen the mainland.

For two years the four men wandered from tribe to tribe, ever westward, more or less following the course of the Rio Grande. Acting as medicine men, they were honored guests of the desert tribes and traveled in comfort. Along the way, Cabeza de Vaca made notes of the wonders he saw—the Plains buffalo, for instance, and the many-storied buildings in Indian pueblos.

Cabeza de Vaca became excited to find some Indians using copper, and he inquired about gold. The Indians waved to the north and said cities of great riches lay that way. He found one tribe with arrowheads of what he thought were emeralds—which they almost certainly were not. The Indians told him again that the emeralds came from rich cities to the north.

Estebanico was a favorite with the Indians, who were fascinated by his dark skin and kinky hair. He enjoyed the role, but Cabeza de Vaca warned him to stay out of Indian affairs lest he stir up trouble.

Almost eight years after landing in Florida, Cabeza de Vaca ran into a Spanish patrol near the modern city of Culiacán on the Pacific Coast of Mexico. In the capital at Mexico City, he told the king's officials the story of his wanderings. He revealed for the first time that the lands north of Florida and Mexico were not scattered islands but a vast unexplored continent with nobody-knew-what treasures hidden there.

Listening to his tales of immensely rich cities north of the Mexican desert, where emeralds were so cheap they could be used for arrowheads, the Spanish planned new expeditions there.

Estebanico went with one of the early expeditions as a guide. He must have been meddling in Indian affairs despite Cabeza de Vaca's warning, for when he appeared before Zuñi pueblo in what is now New Mexico, the guardians of the gates recognized him and on the spot riddled him with arrows. His impact on the Indian imagination was so strong that to this day, almost 450 years later, at most Pueblo ceremonial dances one Indian wears a black face and woolen wig. He dances an eccentric step apart from the others and is called Estebanico.

Almost at the same time, two powerful Spanish armies set out from opposite ends of North America to find those fabled cities of gold hidden somewhere on what Cabeza de Vaca had proved was an immense continent. At Florida in 1539, Hernando de Soto landed almost where Pánfilo de Narváez had landed 11 years earlier. He chased northward the same rumors of gold. Once off the Florida peninsula, he turned westward, wandering through what is now Georgia, Alabama, and Mississippi, torturing Indian chieftains, and ransacking Indian lands in search for gold.

At Culiacán, in 1540, Francisco Vázquez de Coronado set out with 290 Spanish soldiers and 1,000 Indian allies to search for the Seven Cities of Gold Cabeza de Vaca had heard about five years earlier. They wintered at the same Zuñi pueblo where Estebanico had been executed. There Coronado heard from a Plains Indian slave about the rich city of

Quivira far to the northeast. With 30 soldiers and the slave as a guide, he set out in the spring of 1541. He found his Quivira to be a village of huts like Apalachee, and so he killed the slave. At almost the same moment, Hernando de Soto gazed on the Mississippi River near present-day Memphis, the first white man to see the mighty stream.

Chasing away a fleet of menacing Indians from Arkansas, De Soto crossed the river on rafts and continued westward. He may have gone as far as Oklahoma. We know Coronado's Quivira was in Kansas. The two conquistadors may have passed within a few days' march of each other without knowing it.

De Soto turned back to the river and died of a fever on its banks in 1542. Less than half his men straggled home alive. Coronado that same season led only 100 men back into Mexico City. Both expeditions had been disastrous for those involved.

But the lands they crossed became Spanish possessions by right of exploration—Florida, with only occasional brief periods as a British territory, till 1821; most of the Southwest till 1847. The biggest gold mine in North America, ironically, is within a few days' march of the Zuñi pueblo where Coronado spent two winters.

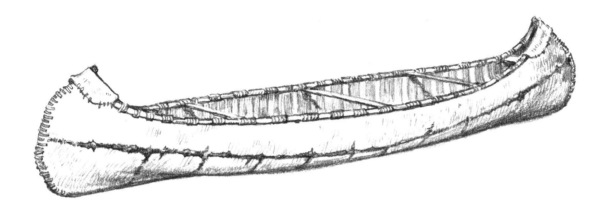

The Great River

A FULL CENTURY after Columbus's landfall in the New World, Europe still cared little about North America north of gold-rich Mexico except as a vexing roadblock across the sea route westward to China. The dream of a Northwest Passage still obsessed Europe's merchants and mariners.

Samuel, Sieur de Champlain, a Frenchman of great curiosity and a high spirit of adventure, went to the Spanish colonies to study the possibility of cutting a canal across the isthmus of Panama at its narrowest part—a plan American engineers achieved three centuries later.

Practical considerations—political and technical—ruled out a Panama Canal in the early 17th century, so Champlain went to French Canada in search of a water route to China. In 1608 he established an Indian trading post on the St. Lawrence River, where now stands the city of Quebec. His backers in France had sent him to make them a fortune in furs, and Champlain meant to carry out his job, but at the same time he pursued that elusive Northwest Passage.

The Indians greedily adopted the goods Champlain offered, throwing away their earthenware pots and stone knives and replacing them with iron kettles that could stand up to any cooking fire and iron blades that could slice the bark from a birch tree with unbelievable speed.

31

After the Iroquois wars, in 1654, the boldest of the *coureurs de bois* headed for the western end of the Great Lakes to resume the fur trade. First among them were Pierre Radisson and his brother-in-law, Médard Chouart, the Sieur de Groseilliers. Reared as a captive of the Iroquois, Radisson was more Indian than white in language and training.

Radisson had deep contempt for the stay-at-home Canadians who made profits from furs without running the woods. He compared their soft life with the hard life of the *coureur de bois*, which he clearly thought more manly.

"It is a different thing when food is wanting, when you work all day and night and lie down on bare ground . . . belly empty and bones weary. . . ."

But Radisson himself was not discouraged by the hard lot of the *coureur*. He and Groseilliers ran the woods freely. They were even more daring woods runners than the Huron Indians, for they had a hard time persuading the Indians to run canoes laden with furs down the Ottawa River to Montreal. The Indians came only after Radisson rigged bales of beaver pelts around the gunwales of the canoes as a bulwark against Iroquois arrows.

Radisson and Groseilliers regularly brought to market tremendous fleets of fur-armored canoes.

As years passed, the Huron refugees became middlemen, trading worn-out iron knives and awls to Plains tribes like the Sioux and the Indians of the North Woods like the Crees for beaver pelts they resold to the French at enormous profit. Radisson and Groseilliers decided to bypass those middlemen and deal directly with the wilder Indians beyond. They particularly liked the furs caught by the Crees in the north country, for the hard winters there forced the furbearers to put on dense, glossy coats of great beauty.

The Crees welcomed the traders with joy and paraded them about the North Woods. Radisson told of that great summer of discovery as guests of the Cree nation.

"We went from isle to isle . . . We were well beloved and the Crees were overjoyed that we promised to come with ships."

Apparently, Radisson had wandered to the shores of Hudson Bay, and he saw instantly the advantages of braving even the terrible ice of that vast frozen inland sea over running canoes through the dangerous

Indian country along the Ottawa River. At least, Radisson *said* he had been to Hudson Bay. Some critics doubted his story then, and some still doubt it. But there is no question of the brilliance of his idea to use the inland sea as a base for loading seagoing ships directly for Europe, thus skipping the dangerous and expensive canoe trip through Iroquois-infested backwoods.

Radisson and Groseilliers returned to Montreal with "so great a number of boats that they almost covered the whole river." It was about 360 boats.

Naturally, they expected to be greeted as heroes—which indeed they were. Instead, the governor tried to hijack legally most of their profits. With disgust, the two *coureurs de bois* deserted their French countrymen and went to New England and finally England. There they sold their scheme of making a great fur empire based on seagoing ships using Hudson Bay for a western base. With the English king's backing, a company of merchants formed the Hudson's Bay Company, which is still in existence as probably the oldest and perhaps the largest trading company in the world.

Thus, one greedy governor in French Canada drove his two best explorers to the British, who not only took home the first load of beaver skins in 1669 but got their foot in the Canadian door, taking over all of Canada, including the French settlements at Montreal and Quebec in 1763.

Champlain had died in 1635, but not his dream of a Northwest Passage. A later French governor hired a *coureur de bois* named Louis Joliet and a Jesuit priest named Jacques Marquette to search for that mysterious Messippi and follow it to the sea. If the sea turned out to be the Pacific, everybody's fortune was made.

In 1672, the fur trader found the priest at the Jesuit mission where Lakes Michigan and Huron join. They set out together on May 17, 1673, to find the Northwest Passage—and of course, to baptize the Indians on the way. Following Nicolet's route, they went up the Fox River. Unlike Nicolet, they crossed the ridge and put their canoes into the Wisconsin. For eight days they paddled down the slow-moving stream. One morning their sluggish river poured into a torrent coming down from the north. The current seized their canoes, and they had to fight their way ashore. They had reached the Mississippi—probably the first white men to see it since De Soto 132 years before.

The explorers knew they had reached the Messippi, the Great River of the Indians, for at that point the Mississippi is a mile wide.

Indians warned them against going downstream, for fear of monsters and ferocious Indian tribes. They continued anyhow and found the monsters harmless enough—huge engravings carved in the rocky bluffs beside the river in what is now Illinois. They were nervous about the Indians and kept Father Marquette clearly visible on the theory that they might not attack a priest—as though those savages knew a Jesuit priest from a subway motorman!

Most of the tribes did treat the voyagers kindly—even too kindly, for they insisted on gorging them with feasts of dogmeat so fat and greasy it turned even the fur trader's stomach.

But near the mouth of the St. Francis River in present-day Arkansas, Indians, perhaps the same tribe that skirmished with De Soto at his river crossing 132 years before, attacked the party. By waving a peace pipe, accepted as sacred protection by almost all Indian tribes, Joliet saved the party. The Indians told him, however, that farther downstream were white men, and to prove it, showed them powder flasks, knives, beads, tomahawks. With one glance, Joliet saw they were Spanish trade goods.

Now he knew the river did not empty into the Pacific, and moreover, he knew he would be a prisoner of war if he fell into Spanish hands. So he and Father Marquette turned back.

By a weird coincidence, they turned back near the same point where De Soto died and his party abandoned their search for gold.

Disappointed that the Mississippi emptied into the Gulf of Mexico, many French Canadians lost interest in the interior. But not Robert Cavelier, Sieur de la Salle, a successful fur trader who had a profitable trading post where Kingston, Ontario, stands today. He saw the Mississippi as a splendid water highway for carrying French trade through the heart of the continent. He would use the river to beat the Dutch and the English to the riches of what the world was now beginning to realize was not a narrow land barrier but a vast continent.

La Salle had a lieutenant named Henri de Tonti, who became one of the most colorful figures of American history. As a soldier in Europe, he had lost one hand in a grenade explosion and had replaced it with an iron hand. Among the Indians, he made a name for being persuasive by bashing his opponent across the head with his iron fist whenever words didn't work.

With a band of Indian allies in 1682, the two fur traders set out to explore the river, looking for sites for a string of French trading posts. After only minor brushes with Indians along the way, they reached the mouth of the river on April 9.

La Salle erected a cross and a post, claiming for the French crown "this land of Louisiana, the seas, harbors, ports, bays, adjacent straits and all the nations, peoples, provinces, cities, towns, villages, mines, minerals, fish, streams and rivers within it." They sang a hymn and fired three volleys to celebrate the day.

La Salle later led a four-ship expedition from France to colonize the mouth of the river, but he missed it by a spectacular number of miles and landed at Matagorda Island in Texas instead—by another weird coincidence, almost exactly where Cabeza de Vaca may have been shipwrecked. One of his own men killed him in 1687, and the colony fell apart.

But by that time the French fur traders and missionaries had opened the continent from the mouth of the St. Lawrence on the Atlantic Coast, through the Great Lakes, and down the Mississippi to the Gulf of Mexico.

The French, long pent up in the East by the Iroquois wars, burst through the openings made by the river explorers. Still using their canoes, they raced through the network of rivers that fed the Mississippi. Father Marquette had been impressed by the mighty flood of the Missouri River and—still pursuing that dream of the Northwest Passage—had suggested that the waterway to the Pacific might lie up that stream.

Far to the north, in 1690, an employee of the new Hudson's Bay Company rambled out into the vast Great Plains and reported a smudge of blue mountains far to the west. Anglo-Saxon historians, almost as quick as the Russians to claim a "first" for their people, have proclaimed this Henry Kelsey as the first white man to see the Rocky Mountains.

But more than fifty years before, the Spanish, as much white men as the English Henry Kelsey, had pushed up from their stable society in Mexico and had established the city of Santa Fe, snuggled 7,000 feet high in the heart of the Rocky Mountains.

In fact, when the first Frenchman went up the Missouri River in 1714 as far as the present South Dakota border, rumors of his travels flew 600 miles across the plains to Santa Fe, where the Spanish governor was filled with alarm at the intrusion on what he considered well-established Spanish territory. That Frenchman was Etienne Veniard de Bourgmond, one of the greatest *coureurs* of all time. Married to an Indian woman, he had an instinctive understanding of Indian psychology and made friends with them easily.

When the Spanish sent out a 110-man cavalry column to root out the Frenchman, Bourgmond had done his homework so well that the Pawnee Indians took his side and smashed the Spaniards, killing almost half the column and sending the others reeling back to Santa Fe.

So confident were the French of their hold on the Plains Indians that two brothers, Pierre and Paul Mallet, followed the road of the Spaniards from Bourgmond's post to Santa Fe, where they did a little trading before turning homeward.

Shortly after the Mallet trip, the Spanish colonized what is now Texas beginning at San Antonio in 1714, partly because the French were crowding ever closer around the Gulf shore with colonies planted by the great adventurer Pierre le Moyne, Sieur d'Iberville, at Biloxi in 1699 and by his brother Jean Baptiste, Sieur de Bienville, at New Orleans in 1718.

The Mallet voyage and the founding of the Gulf Coast and Texas cities closed a grand circle of explored lands from Florida up the Atlantic Coast to Canada, across the Great Lakes country, southwestward across the Great Plains to Santa Fe, and from there back eastward through Texas and the Louisiana shore.

But in the heart of that great circle lay a vast, supposedly unknown space, the region between the crest of the Appalachian Mountains and the Mississippi River. Actually, many *coureurs de bois* from French trading posts along the Mississippi and Illinois rivers had been struggling there to hold on to their fur trade with the Indians. They had discovered competition from Dutch and English fur traders who crossed the mountains to claim the Ohio basin. In fact, struggle for those trading rights helped bring on the French and Indian wars.

When all of French Louisiana and Canada, except for New Orleans, went to Great Britain in 1763, the *coureurs de bois* had to switch their trade to British forts—a switch they performed easily because they felt little loyalty to anybody but themselves anyhow. They had good reason for their easy change of loyalty, because their French bosses had cheated them as a matter of routine.

The fur traders—British, Dutch, and former French—traveled widely across that rich basin land, but settlers on the increasingly crowded Atlantic Coast still felt shut off by the mountain range.

The Long Hunters

UNLIKE THE FRENCH of Canada and the Mississippi Valley, the settlers of the English colonies along the Atlantic Coast had no rivers to carry canoes deep into the interior. Just inland from the coast rose the Appalachian mountain chain, blocking the way west. Any explorers of the far side of the mountains would have to go on foot, wherever they could find a gap.

Those gaps, remarkably few in that 1,500-mile-long wall, were found —naturally—by fur traders, and most of them were French *coureurs de bois*, to boot. (The occasional Dutch fur traders were called *boschlopers*, which means precisely the same thing—"woods runners.")

After La Salle's murder in 1687, Henri de Tonti of the Iron Hand had tried to rescue the French colony on Matagorda Island in the midst of hostile Indian and Spanish country. But he was too late. The fort had been destroyed, and the colonists killed or scattered among the tribes. (Two of the youngsters captured there, the Talon brothers, were reared as Indians, then ransomed and adopted by the wife of the Mexican viceroy and educated at the brilliant viceregal court in the Mexican capital. On their way to Spain they were captured by the French, and they enlisted in an expedition to the Mississippi. They spent some time in prison in Portugal and made their way back to Louisiana, where they became among the most daring explorers in the history of southwestern North America. Surely, the life story of the Talon brothers is one of the most exciting ever to come from the American frontier.)

Tonti went back to the Mississippi Valley and set about establishing the chain of forts and trading stations his dead leader had planned. One of his outposts was near the mouth of the Arkansas River—by another co-incidence, not far from the place where De Soto had died and Joliet and Marquette had turned back. Among Tonti's most able *coureurs de bois* there was a Jean Couture.

Sometime before 1700, Jean Couture deserted the French and rambled the woods of the Upper South between the Mississippi and the Appalachians, doing his own trading and pocketing all the profits. He crossed the mountains into South Carolina. When local businessmen heard his tales of the rich country across the Appalachians, they organized a party, in 1700, and hired him to lead them through the gaps he had found.

Farther north, in 1750, a Dr. Thomas Walker went on a surveying trip through the Cumberland Gap, the main pass through the mountains leading from North Carolina and Virginia into Kentucky and Tennessee. The next year a Christopher Gist blazed a trail from the Potomac River, which empties into the Atlantic, to a tributary of the Ohio River, which empties into the Gulf of Mexico by way of the Mississippi. They are often credited with having discovered those mountain passes.

But they freely admitted that they found the way blazed, with hundreds of trees marked by the tomahawks of fur traders who had been crossing those mountains for years.

And those trappers brought back tales of the fertility of the Kentucky basin that set afire the land greed of the small farmers on the Atlantic side of the mountains. Wild stories circulated about the "earthly paradise" just beyond the passes. There, it was spring the year round; tree limbs broke under the load of wild turkeys roosting for the night; deer and buffalo crowded hunters off the forest trails. And the dense cane-brakes and lofty forests showed how fertile was the soil, how ready for the planter's plow.

In 1766, a Benjamin Cutbird led a hunting party not only across the mountains into the Mississippi Valley but clean across Kentucky and Tennessee, then floated down to New Orleans to sell his tremendous catch of furs.

Among his men was a John Stewart, who went back to the Yadkin River valley in North Carolina and told his hunter's tales to Daniel Boone. He could not have found a better audience, for Daniel had spent his 32 years drifting about from one frontier farm to another, halfheartedly raising a crop of corn during the summer and slipping off into the woods with the first snow to spend the winter hunting and trapping. Like most frontiersmen, Daniel had a passion for the woods life.

Years before, he had served as a wagoner with General Braddock's frontier expedition, the same disastrous parade through the forest that was ambushed by French and Indians and whose retreat was led by George Washington after the general's death. Before the disaster, around the campfires, Daniel had heard John Finley, a trapper, tell tales of the rich bluegrass country in Kentucky and a wide gap in the mountains. John Stewart's stories excited Daniel again. To get supplies, he went to a land speculator named Judge Richard Henderson, who financed his explorations in exchange for advance knowledge of the best sites to be snapped up when Daniel found a road west.

During the winter of 1767–68, Daniel crossed the mountains but picked the wrong gap and came out in a rough wilderness nothing like the rich country Finley had described. He went home in the spring with a treasure in furs but no knowledge of the bluegrass country. Before he could set out again the next fall, a peddler dropped into the Yadkin Valley. Daniel and the peddler leaped on each other at sight, slapping each other on the back and hallooing with joy.

It was John Finley. He needed no persuasion to dump his pack of needles and cloth in Daniel's cabin and set out with him in search of the road to the bluegrass. Finley had never been to Cumberland Gap, but his trapper friends had described it carefully, and he was sure he could find it.

In 1769 the party set out on ponies—Finley and Boone with four other woodsmen, including the John Stewart whose tales of his trip to the Mississippi and New Orleans had excited Daniel.

Finley found Cumberland Gap easily, and they rode into Kentucky. They built a cabin to protect the furs they had already taken, and they split up into small parties to explore the region faster.

Daniel and Finley stayed together. A band of Shawnee warriors captured them and stole all the furs and supplies cached in the cabin. The Indian warriors glutted themselves on the explorers' supplies and fell into a heavy sleep. The two frontiersmen slipped away in the darkness and hid in a canebrake till the raiding party had left.

When the rest of the party gathered about the looted cabin, they were so discouraged they all went home except for Stewart and Daniel. Shortly thereafter Daniel's brother Squire joined them with a single companion.

During the next winter, Stewart went off on a hunting trip and never returned. Squire's companion gave up and went home. The two brothers hung on for a while, but Squire finally decided to go home for more ammunition. Daniel was left alone in the Kentucky wilderness.

For months, Daniel rambled through the woods, hunting and trapping. Having once been captured by a Shawnee hunting party, he did not trust his chances of escaping a second time, so he slept hidden deep in canebrakes. When he had to shoot his rifle, he melted into the woods for a while to be sure he had not attracted the attention of a band of Indians.

Wandering alone, he explored the banks of the Ohio, Kentucky, and Licking rivers and most of the rich bluegrass region. He rejoined his brother in July at the old campsite. Already he knew more about Kentucky than any other living man, red or white. But Daniel and his brother stayed on through another winter.

Only once did he relax his guard, and he was caught. Filled with joy at being in the wilderness he loved, he threw himself to the ground under a tree and lay on his back singing. He apparently had more luck than voice, for he did call attention to himself by his reckless bawling—but it was a party of white hunters who heard him, and they thought it was an animal caterwauling. Daniel and his brother joined the party for the winter trapping. For the next several months they explored the Green and Cumberland valleys.

In March 1771 they were ready to go home with a small fortune in furs gathered during two years of hard work. Near Cumberland Gap, however, the fate Daniel had avoided for two years caught up with them. A band of Indians captured them and took away their furs, horses, and supplies. The brothers had to walk home with nothing to show for their hard work and dangerous adventures . . . nothing, that is, but the widest knowledge of the bluegrass country of any men on earth.

Daniel's backer, Judge Henderson, got plans under way immediately to make use of Daniel's knowledge.

OVERLEAF: *American Frontier Life* By Arthur Tait
YALE UNIVERSITY ART GALLERY, WHITNEY COLLECTIONS OF SPORTING ART,
given in memory of Harry Payne Whitney (B.A. 1894) and
Payne Whitney (B.A. 1898) by Francis P. Garvan (B.A. 1897)

First came the problem of the Indians. The powerful Cherokees living south of Kentucky and the Shawnees in the north apparently had some kind of agreement to leave the region uninhabited as a vast game preserve visited only by hunting parties. Though they did not live there, they felt they shared ownership of the country.

So Daniel went first to the Cherokees and in 1775 traded a few wagonloads of guns, tools, cloth, and trinkets for two million acres of land. Daniel and Judge Henderson neglected to deal with the Shawnees, because they had already been mauled by an army expedition sent from Pittsburgh and had promised not to molest settlers.

Then Daniel led a work party to cut a trail 300 miles through the forest to the Kentucky River. The trail became famous as the Wilderness Road.

Cutting that trail was like pulling the cork from a jug. Settlers poured through the gap to take up lands on the west side of the mountains. Daniel and his party built a fort and cabins at Boonesboro. (Another band of settlers had built a fort at nearby Harrodsburg. The village and fort have been rebuilt as a charming museum of frontier life.)

The Shawnees were outraged when they found their hunting grounds being cleared of trees and turned by plows. Forgetting the beating the army had given them, they attacked settlers across the whole frontier.

Daniel's 14-year-old daughter, Jemima, and two companions were kidnapped by a band of Shawnees led by a Cherokee named Hanging Jowls. Daniel organized a posse and raced ahead of the Indians. He laid an ambush, surprised the Indians, and drove them off. The girls went back home unharmed.

Back east, the Revolutionary War had broken out, but across the mountains in Kentucky it made only the faintest echo. Except that the British at Detroit did use the Indians to harass the American frontier—which included Boonesboro, of course.

For the third time in his life, Daniel was kidnapped by Shawnees, and he was taken by Chief Blackfish to the British fort. General Hamilton offered Blackfish 100 pounds for his captive, but the Indian refused. Instead, he took Daniel to his camp near present-day Chillicothe, Ohio, and adopted him as his son. Daniel apparently did not return the affection, especially after he heard the young braves planning an attack on his own town of Boonesboro.

Daniel escaped at night and crossed the flooded Ohio River in a canoe.

In the next four days he traveled 160 miles, an astonishing trip for a man crossing a wilderness on foot.

When 400 Shawnees attacked the fort, they found 40 Kentucky frontiersmen ready with their deadly long rifles poked through loopholes in the stockade wall. Pioneer women loaded weapons and carried water. When burning arrows landed on the roof, men exposed themselves to Indian fire while they beat out the flames. The Indians showed amazing military sophistication by digging a tunnel under the walls for exploding a gunpowder mine. Still the frontiersmen held them off.

Brave enough to stand up against the rifle fire of the world's best marksmen, the Shawnees broke off their attack when a thunderstorm drenched their buckskins. They fled into the forest.

Like many another frontiersman, Boone woke up one day to discover that other men who knew their way around a courtroom as well as he knew the wilderness had taken legal possession of the lands he thought were his. Game was getting scarce anyhow, so in 1799, Daniel, at 65 no longer a young woods runner, moved across the Mississippi River into what was then Spanish Louisiana and is now Missouri. He lived a quiet life there—except for a trip to the Yellowstone in the Rocky Mountains—till he died at the age of 86.

Daniel had lived long enough to see himself become a legend as the model long hunter, the ideal frontiersman. He was the hero of several poems and epics by Europe's greatest writers.

Death of the Northwest Passage

BY THE EARLY 18TH CENTURY, the Atlantic Coast of North America had filled with settlers to the point that the land-hungry were pressing against the mountain barrier looking for a way to the unclaimed lands of the interior. But the Pacific Coast remained virtually unknown. As the 18th century opened, nobody except a few Eskimos even knew if Asia and North America were joined in the far northwest like Siamese twins or if they were separate continents. As early as 1648 a great Russian sailor named Simon Dezhnev had sailed from the Siberian coast of the Arctic sea through the straits between the two continents, but his report was lost in the red tape of the Russian court. It was not till Vitus Bering, a Danish sailor hired by the Russians, repeated Dezhnev's voyage in 1741 that the world learned the approximate shape of Alaska.

Of far more interest to the world's traders than the separation of the continents was the fortune in sea-otter furs to be made in those Alaskan waters. After centuries of neglect, Spanish, British, and Dutch governments sent ships to map the Pacific Coast of North America. Within a very few years of Bering's voyages, those exploring seamen found Russians trading for furs as far south as Fort Ross, near present-day San Francisco.

Those Russians sold their furs in China for immense profits. News of that rich trade spread across North America, exciting merchants with the possibility of finding that elusive Northwest Passage through which to carry their pelts from the interior of North America to the Pacific. *Voyageurs*—as the *coureurs de bois* became known when they left eastern forests for the western plains—had sliced across North America everywhere south of what is now the Canadian border, and they had reported no gap through the mountains leading to the Pacific. If a Northwest Passage existed anywhere, it lay in the north, probably stretching from somewhere on Hudson Bay to the Pacific somewhere in Alaska.

In 1783, a group of merchants formed the North West Company to compete with the Hudson's Bay Company in the fur trade on the western prairies and forests. Their traders were young and aggressive, but the company had a serious disadvantage. They could not use the shortcut to the sea that Radisson and Groseilliers had given to the British, the route through Hudson Bay. The North West Company had to send its furs to Europe by a roundabout southern route. So the young agents on the prairies talked endlessly about finding a river leading to the Pacific as a shortcut to the Chinese market and even greater profits than were to be made in Europe.

Among the young traders who gossiped around the campfires about a river to the Pacific was a Scotsman named Alexander Mackenzie. On Lake Athabasca, Mackenzie met a Connecticut trader who had built a post there. This Peter Pond had explored farther into the surrounding wilderness than any other white man. He firmly believed that the great river leading north out of Lake Athabasca ran to the Pacific.

So, early in June 1789, Mackenzie, who was only 25 years old, left the lake in two canoes with five *voyageurs*, two Indian women, an Indian guide, some Indian hunters, a supply of pemmican—as dried meat and fat was called—and trade goods for dealing with Indians along the way. He crossed the Great Slave Lake through broken ice just beginning to thaw and for six days probed at the western bank looking for an outlet. When he found a broad river flowing westward, Mackenzie steered his flotilla into the stream, hoping that the course ran steadily westward to the Pacific as a broad avenue to carry the company's furs to the Chinese market.

But early in July the river met a range of mountains blocking the way and it turned northward. Mackenzie followed the river, hoping it would find a notch in the mountains and turn westward again. But it poured its torrent steadily northward. They voyaged far beyond the limits of previous voyages, and Indians along the banks stared openmouthed at the strange white skin of Mackenzie and his *voyageurs*. They warned him of monsters downstream and said he would be an old man before he returned from the river's mouth. He sailed even beyond Indian country into the land of the Eskimos, where Indians did not dare venture. On July 10, he reached the sea, but Mackenzie realized with sinking heart that the ice-choked waste stretching northward was not the Pacific but the Arctic Ocean.

He named the stream River Disappointment and turned back. The party arrived home 102 days and 2,750 miles after leaving. Mackenzie did not know it, but he had explored a stream that became the major roadway for Canadian fur traffic. Today it bears his name and is the longest river in Canada.

Mackenzie did not give up on his plan to explore a route to the Pacific, but he returned to England first and studied surveying and geography so that he could give a solid scientific foundation to further travels.

During his voyage down the Mackenzie, the young Scot had heard from Indians about a great river to the west with Russian traders along its banks. We know now it was the Yukon River, but Mackenzie hoped it was his long-sought river to the Pacific much farther south.

This time, in 1793, Mackenzie headed west on the Peace River, leading out of Lake Athabasca. In his party were seven *voyageurs* and two Indians. They carried 3,000 pounds of supplies in a 25-foot canoe so cleverly designed that two men could carry it for three or four hours without tiring. When the explorers paddled away from their base camp at the forks of the Peace and Smoky rivers, the men who were left behind to guard the fort burst into tears.

Within two days the current had grown so strong the *voyageurs* had to give up paddling and begin pushing the canoe upstream by poling. They ran into a camp of Indians who trotted along the banks talking to Mackenzie's hunters and trying to persuade them not to go farther into the unexplored mountains. But Mackenzie pushed on.

Game was so numerous that Mackenzie said the plains looked like a barnyard. He also saw "two grizzly and hideous bears."

On May 17, the party saw the Rocky Mountains—"their summits covered with snow." Even in the lowlands it froze almost every night, though it was mid-May.

Progress on the river was halted by rapids and waterfalls, forcing the party to unload the canoe and carry it and the supplies upstream. In some of the swiftest waters they towed the canoe by long ropes. Powerful currents drove the canoe against the rocks and punctured the hull, causing long delays for repairs.

Rocky cliffs forced them to cross to the other bank by canoe, a daring undertaking, for the rushing torrent almost carried them over a waterfall to certain death.

The river became so wild that in a space of two miles they had to load and unload the canoe four times to carry it around rapids. Finally, the river became one continuous rapids. Mackenzie reported his dismay on looking upstream.

". . . the river above us, as far as we could see, was one white sheet of foaming water . . . it began to be muttered on all sides that there was no alternative but to return."

Mackenzie ordered his men to the top of the cliff to make camp, and he went exploring upstream on foot. He found no end to the dangerous torrent and decided they would have to continue on foot. He set his men to hacking a road through the underbrush that covered the mountainside. Then they dragged their supplies and the canoe over the mountain at the end of towropes. Beginning at four o'clock in the morning, the men labored mightily till sunset—and made good three miles. The next day they crossed a *brule*, a section burned out by a forest fire and grown up again in dense brush, thorn trees, and briers. They made good four miles. To explain why he chose to hack his way so painfully over a mountain instead of poling his canoe up the river, Mackenzie described the stream.

". . . the channel widens in a kind of zig-zag progression; and it was really awful to behold with what infinite force the water drives against the rocks on one side, and with what impetuous strength it is repelled to the other: it then falls back . . . into a more strait but rugged passage, over which it is tossed in high, foaming, half-formed billows, as far as the eye could follow it."

The *voyageurs* found heaps of wood cut by axes, so they knew that Indians who had been trading with white men had been around. To a pole, Mackenzie lashed a knife, beads, and other gifts and planted it, hoping the Indians would accept the presents as a sign of friendship.

They walked far enough upstream to find smooth water and put

OVERLEAF: *Up-River Men*
By Frederic Remington
COURTESY OF REMINGTON ART MUSEUM,
OGDENSBURG, NEW YORK

out again in their canoe. Though they worked hard poling the boat, the mountain air was so keen they had to put on their winter coats.

On June 9 a rainstorm drove them ashore to make camp. But they smelled fresh smoke from a wood fire and heard sounds of people thrashing about in the woods in apparent confusion. They guessed correctly that they had stumbled on an Indian party and had thrown them into an uproar. Not knowing how hostile they were, Mackenzie had his men paddle to the other shore.

Two Indians came out of the woods, waving their lances and bows and calling threats. Mackenzie's Indians told them the party came in peace, but they threatened to attack if Mackenzie tried to cross the stream to their side.

"I readily complied with their proposition," Mackenzie said.

Finally convinced of Mackenzie's peaceful mission, they allowed him to cross. They had never seen white men before, so they examined the whites and their equipment in the tiniest detail. Mackenzie sent one of the men to bring back the party that had scattered in the woods when they first saw the whites. The other Indian he kept as a hostage to guarantee peace.

Mackenzie wanted to gain their friendship so that he could learn from them where to portage across the mountains and find a river running down to the Pacific on the far side.

The Indians did report that they traded with tribes that traded with white men on the Pacific, but they denied any knowledge of how to find a river running that way. Mackenzie, however, suspected that his interpreter was sick of the trip and not translating all he heard so as to discourage the boss and persuade him to turn back. So Mackenzie plied the Indians with gifts and kindness and hung about eavesdropping as they chatted with his hunters. Though he was not fluent in the language, he had picked up enough so that he hoped to surprise any secret exchange of knowledge.

Next morning he did, indeed, catch an Indian telling a hunter about a river across the mountain that ran south but did not empty into the sea. He drew a map on a bit of bark with a piece of charcoal. Mackenzie did not believe the business about not emptying into the sea, for it is a rare river that does not lead to the sea sooner or later.

Also, he was struck by how many iron instruments the Indians had —two kinds of spearpoints, adzes, arrowheads, knives. From that, Mackenzie decided the difficulty of reaching the trading posts on the Pacific was not so great as the Indians pretended.

One of the mountain Indians went with the party as a guide.

He led them across the ridge and down a string of lakes to a river running in a promising direction. So began again the process of floating till they reached rapids and hacking their way through the woods around the rapids. The Indian guide was scared by the recklessness of the *voyageurs*. And he had good reason, for the canoe hit a rock and fell apart, dumping them all into the frigid stream. They barely made it to shore, where they discovered they had lost all their bullets.

Mackenzie reported that his men were not all upset by the accident.

"Indeed, when my people began to recover from their alarm and to enjoy a sense of safety, some of them, if not all, were by no means sorry for our late misfortune, from the hope that it must put a period to our voyage, particularly as we were without a canoe, and all the bullets sunk in the river."

But Mackenzie pointed out that they had saved the gunpowder and the buckshot which they could melt and cast into bullets. As for the wrecked canoe, he reminded them that any *voyageur* worthy of the name could make a canoe from scratch wherever he could find birchbark, and so he could certainly repair a wrecked canoe.

But progress down their tributary, even when they had patched the canoe, was more of the old business of floating a while and then hacking a path for a portage. And the canoe was so heavy with patches that four men could carry it no farther than 100 yards at a time.

Just before sunset they finally reached the great river, a navigable river running down the west side of the mountains toward the sea. Mackenzie thought he had reached the Columbia River, which mariners had visited at its mouth on the Pacific, but he was on the Fraser River. He did not follow it downstream but struck across the country. He reached the Pacific Ocean near the north tip of Vancouver Island in modern-day British Columbia on July 22, 1793.

Thus, for the first time in history a man had traveled overland from sea to sea, crossing the entire North American continent.

What Have We Bought?

AS THE 19TH CENTURY opened, Europe was in even more turmoil than usual. Napoleon had taken over the French Revolution, and most of the kings had lined up against him. Spain had long held what was then called Louisiana, roughly the lands west of the Mississippi River to the Rocky Mountains. But Spain had ruled the territory in name only. The settlers were a mixture of French fur traders and a very few Americans like Daniel Boone.

In one of the complicated deals that tormented Europe during the Napoleonic wars, the French ruler took Louisiana from Spain and almost immediately sold it to the infant United States. With a scratch of the pen, the young nation acquired an immense stretch of fertile valley and grassy plain. And very literally nobody knew exactly what the country had bought, because no white man had seen most of it. And the boundaries were vague. Nobody was sure where English territory left off along the northern border and where Spanish territory stopped on the west and southwest.

Knowing that the presence of a band of armed men waving the flag was a strong argument, President Thomas Jefferson decided to send a party westward across the newly bought Louisiana Territory and beyond, all the way to the Pacific. Their job was to find out what was out there—for truly no living man knew what wonders they would find or even how far they would have to travel to reach the sea. They also had the job of showing the American flag on the Pacific Coast to establish the American claim and cut off Russian and British expansion southward along that shore.

But the main purpose was to hunt for that same old Northwest Passage that had lured explorers of North America for 300 years or at least a westward-running river with only a short portage from the headwaters of an eastward-running river.

When Thomas Jefferson named his secretary, U.S. Army Capt. Meriwether Lewis, chief of an expedition to explore the Louisiana Territory, he made it clear that the search for the Northwest Passage was his first job.

"The object of your mission is to explore the Missouri river, & such principal stream of it, as, by it's course & communication with the waters of the Pacific Ocean, may offer the most direct & practicable water communication across this continent, for the purposes of commerce."

By then, geographers knew that no single river ran across the continent, but Jefferson asked Lewis to find the best portage between the headwaters of the Missouri and the headwaters of a river flowing in the other direction toward the Pacific. For the president hoped to find a water route with only a small land break that would do away with the long, expensive trip by ship from the United States ports of the Atlantic Coast around the tip of South America and north to the trading posts of the Pacific Northwest. Lewis was also told to note the customs, languages, possibilities for trade among the Indians, and the climate and unknown animals and plants.

Captain Lewis, joined by Capt. William Clark, also of the U.S. Army, gathered forces on the east bank of the Mississippi near St. Louis in the winter of 1803–04. (The Spanish governor in St. Louis had not yet been told about the Louisiana Purchase and would not let them use what he considered Spanish soil for their camp. Early next spring, he learned that Spain had lost Louisiana and he had lost a job.)

Besides Lewis and Clark, the party included fourteen army volunteers, nine young Kentucky long hunters, and two *voyageurs.* All were enlisted as privates. Captain Clark also had a black servant named York, an uncommonly powerful man whose great muscles caused much comment among the Indians. The captains named three sergeants from among the privates.

Another party of a corporal and six soldiers and nine *voyageurs* would go with them as far as the Mandan nation in modern-day North Dakota, supposedly the farthest point of western exploration by anybody, American or English. They were to travel in a 55-foot-long keelboat with square sail and 22 oars. Fore and aft cabins offered some protection from the weather, and along the sides lockers could be swung up as protection against Indian arrows. For light river duties, they were taking two small open boats. Two horses were to follow along the banks for use as hunters or dray horses.

Lewis told about the events of that first crossing of the United States.

"...we left our encampment on Monday, May 14th, 1804."

On May 25, they passed La Charrette, a village of seven small houses "and as many poor families who have fixed themselves here for the convenience of trade and form the last establishment of whites on the Missouri."

They had passed the last white village, but they continued to pass rafts and canoes loaded down with furs that traders had bought from the Plains Indians. Some of the traders had been months on the way downstream.

Along the way, they found ruins of forts and villages where French traders had once lived. And once in a while they met traders headed for St. Louis with a load of furs. They even persuaded one of them, who had known the Sioux tribe for years, to go back upriver with them as a go-between.

At a powwow with Oto tribal chieftains, including one named Big Horse and another with the less heroic name of Little Thief, a present was given to one of the subchiefs whose name indicates that white fur traders had indeed crisscrossed that land for many years. He was called Great Blue Eyes.

Near a village of the Iowa Indians the next day, Sgt. Charles Floyd collapsed with what Lewis called a "bilious cholic."

"I am going to leave you," the sergeant said and died.

He was buried and his grave marked by a cedar post replaced generations later by a tall column honoring him as the first U.S. Army soldier to die west of the Mississippi. He died near present-day Sioux City, Iowa.

Farther along, Lewis was amused by the superstitious fear of the neighboring Indians for a rectangular-shaped hillock in the plain. They said it was home to dwarflike devils, 18 inches high, who shot down foolish Indians wandering too close to the sacred heap. Lewis describes the little mountain. Today we can recognize it as indeed a sacred place for the Indians, for he gives a perfect description of a temple pyramid of the Mound Builders, those prehistoric Indians who once brought a kind of civilization to the Mississippi-Missouri basin.

Lewis sent his sergeants and experienced traders on side trips to inform the Indians of the change of ownership of Louisiana from Spain to America. Those messengers often were offered a roast fat dog as a sign of friendship, and they reported it pretty good eating.

Along the riverbanks, they inspected ruins of Indian fortifications, for they were entering Sioux country, and the Sioux were among the very few North American Indians who built earthworks like European armies. One that they inspected enclosed 20 acres, making it a bigger fortress than almost any in medieval Europe. At least, Lewis thought the formations were ruined fortresses, though some so-called experts who weren't there ridicule the idea and say they were merely ordinary erosions. (Yet, another army explorer, Lt. Zebulon Pike, the following year reported seeing Sioux Indians frantically digging fortifications in the plains when they thought their enemies the Chippewas were about to attack.)

On September 25, 1804, the captains held a powwow with the Sioux chieftains on the riverbank. They invited the chieftains aboard the keelboat and gave them a drink of whiskey. The Indians did not want to leave, but Captain Clark finally took them ashore in the small boat, with five of his men as a bodyguard. He had been wise to bring some men with him, for three Indians grabbed the towrope of the boat to hold it inshore, and another wrapped his arms around the mast. A young chief complained that he had not received enough presents and said the white men could not go back to the keelboat till he was paid off. It was exactly that kind of bullying the army was supposed to prevent.

Lewis, watching from the keelboat, reports what happened.

" . . . captain Clark told him . . . that we were not squaws, but warriors; that we were sent by our great father, who could in a moment exterminate them: the chief replied, that he too had warriors, and was proceeding to offer personal violence to captain Clark, who immediately drew his sword. . . . The Indians who surrounded him, drew their arrows from their quivers and were bending their bows, when the swivel in the boat was instantly pointed towards them, and twelve of our most determined men . . . joined Captain Clark."

Lewis and Clark Meeting the Indians at Ross' Hole
By Charles M. Russell

A swivel was a kind of super sawed-off shotgun, a bell-mouthed, small cannon loaded with musket balls and buckshot. At that close range, a single blast from that terrible blunderbuss would have torn bloody holes in the ranks of the Sioux. Looking toward the keelboat, the hot-blooded warriors were chilled to see they were looking down the barrels of a rank of rifles poked through slits in the locker-box barricade along the sides. The Sioux had never before met a band of travelers so difficult to scare. So they withdrew a short distance and huddled to decide their next move. Captain Clark walked up to the Indians, trying to shake hands, but they refused. He returned to his boat, but he had hardly turned his back before the two chiefs and two warriors ran after him and climbed into the boat as friends.

Captain Clark's sword, the swivel gun, and the rank of long rifles pointing from the keelboat impressed the Sioux, for the next morning they gave a grand banquet of state for the explorers, smoking the peace pipe and serving roast dog in vast amounts.

The party still ran into French traders, so white skin was no novelty to those Indians, but the black man, York, caused much excitement when they reached the country of the Arikara tribe. Captain Clark (whose powers of spelling were feeble) reported one of the visits in his journal.

"many Came to view us all day, much astonished at my black Servent, who did not lose the opportunity of (displaying) his powers Strength &c, &c, this nation never Saw a black man before."

York apparently enjoyed the attention and pretended to be ferocious. The next day at a council of chiefs, he was the hit of the show. Captain Clark reports:

"Those Indians wer much astonished at my Servent, they never Saw a black man before, all flocked around him & examind him from top to toe, he Carried on the joke and make himself more turribal than we wished him to doe."

Captain Lewis court-martialed a soldier for disobeying orders, had him flogged with 75 lashes, and sent him back to St. Louis. An Arikara chieftain who witnessed the whipping was horrified. He said he understood the need for punishment and had himself killed criminals, but he said "his nation never whipped even children from their birth."

From the Arikara country, the party entered the lands of the Mandan Indians, a strange tribe that had always stirred up great interest among the whites. The first French trading expeditions to the upper

Missouri River decades before had been sent to seek out a tribe of supposedly white-skinned Indians—these same Mandans. The Mandans crossed streams in a round bullboat similar to the curraghs used by the Welsh and Irish people. Somebody started the story that they were the lost Welshmen who had come to America in the 12th century with Prince Madoc—the same legendary party honored by the Daughters of the American Revolution with a plaque on the shores of Mobile Bay in Alabama.

A few years before the Lewis and Clark expedition, a Welsh-speaking trader named John Evans had visited the Mandans and had left them in disgust because he could not understand a word of their language. They were not the Welsh Indians, of course, but they were a powerful and fairly civilized tribe with a culture somewhat more advanced than the nomadic tribes around them. They also were the farthest west of any Indians ever visited by white men, even by French *voyageurs*, on the western plains. So Lewis and Clark were nearing the beginning of the unknown.

November had come, and in the northern Great Plains snow falls early. The captains decided to winter with the Indians, and so they built a blockhouse they called Fort Mandan.

At the fort on February 11, 1805, an event happened that seemed insignificant at the time but that became very important to the expedition. Sacajawea, the Indian wife of a *voyageur* named Toussaint Charbonneau, gave birth to a son. This Sacajawea was not a Mandan, but a Shoshone from far to the west. She had been captured during one of the endless intertribal wars, but still considered herself a Shoshone, knew the Shoshone country, and spoke the language. The two captains wisely invited her to go with the expedition in the spring, and she proved to be invaluable as an interpreter and guide. She carried her papoose on a board strapped to her back. Wherever they went through Indian country, the baby amused the Indians and often prevented bloodshed, for Indians never took their squaws and babies when they went on the warpath. The baby on his mother's back was the best guarantee possible that the explorers came in peace.

A few days later they learned that the North West Company had merged with the XY Company, and the new company was headed by the great Alexander Mackenzie. The news was alarming, for it meant that the British in Canada would make a hard drive to reach the mouth of the Columbia River on the Pacific shore and claim land far south of where the Americans wished the Canadian border to stop. The merger forced the expedition to hurry their departure from Fort Mandan.

The men spent the winter building six dugouts made of cottonwood logs to replace the heavy keelboat, for the river became too shallow beyond Fort Mandan for deep-draft vessels. On April 7, 1805, Captain Lewis sent the keelboat back to St. Louis. He also sent his notebooks to be relayed to President Jefferson, so that if he and his party should be lost on the second half of the trip, the first half would still be a profit to the United States. Two Arikara chiefs also went downstream toward St. Louis with the idea of visiting President Jefferson in Washington.

The rest of the party pushed off in the six dugouts and two larger boats, heading upstream into country never before explored by white men. Captain Lewis wrote in his journal:

"This little fleet altho' not quite so rispectable as those of Columbus or Capt. Cook, were still viewed by us with as much pleasure as those deservedly famed adventurers ever beheld theirs; and I dare say with quite as much anxiety for their safety and preservation. we were now about to penetrate a country at least two thousand miles in width, on which the foot of civilized man had never trodden; the good or evil it had in store for us was . . . yet to determine."

Despite those brave words about entering country where civilized men had never been, they still ran into French traders, who joined them for a short stretch on their way to the mouth of the Yellowstone River, the main tributary of the Missouri. Of all the explorers of North America, surely the bravest and ablest were the *coureurs de bois* and the *voyageurs,* who always seemed to be well established on the scene when the so-called first white men arrived there. And yet we know the names today of only a few of the thousands that roamed the wilderness where even the Indians would not go with them.

Tracks of the grizzly bear became more frequent, and the men eagerly watched for their first glimpse of the silver-tipped giants, despite Indian warnings of their ferocious nature. Captain Lewis recorded the respect the Indians felt for what they called the "white bear."

"The Indians . . . never dare to attack but in parties of six eight or ten persons; and are even then frequently defeated with the loss of one or more of their party. The savages attack this anamal with their bows and arrows and the indifferent guns with which the traders furnish them, with these they shoot with such uncertainty and at so short a distance

that . . . they frequently mis their aim and fall a sacrefice to the bear.
this anamall is said more frequently to attack a man on meeting with
him, than to flee from him."

On June 13, 1805, they came to the Great Falls of the Missouri,
where the river cascaded 80 feet, forcing an exhausting portage that took
days. While the men were carrying supplies and boats around the falls,
Captain Lewis went hunting. He wounded a buffalo and was watching
him bleed, waiting for him to fall. He didn't bother to reload his rifle, for
he expected the bull to die any moment. He happened to glance behind
himself and froze with horror.

"A large bear had perceived and crept up on me within 20 steps before I discovered him; in the first moment I drew up my gun to shoot,
but at the same instant recolected that she was not loaded and that he
was too near for me to hope to perform this opperation before he reached
me, as he was then briskly advancing on me; it was an open level plain,
not a bush within miles nor a tree within less than three hundred yards
of me; the river bank was sloping and not more than three feet above

the level of the water; in short there was no place by means of which I could conceal myself from this monster untill I could charge my rifle; . . . I thought of retreating in a brisk walk . . . as he was advancing untill I could reach a tree about 300 yards below me, but I had no sooner terned myself about but he pitched at me, open mouthed and full speed, I ran about 80 yards and found he gained on me fast, I then run into the water the idea struk me to get into the water to such debth that I could stand and he would be obliged to swim, and that I could . . . defend myself with my espontoon [a short spear Captain Lewis always carried to use as a rest for his rifle while aiming]. accordingly I ran haistily into the water about waist deep, and faced about and presented the point of my espontoon. at this instant he arrived at the edge of the water within about 20 feet of me; the moment I put myself in this attitude of defence he sudonly wheeled about . . . declined to combat on such unequal grounds and retreated."

On climbing out from the water, Captain Lewis reloaded his rifle and never again ventured out with an unloaded gun.

At Three Forks, three small rivers come together to form the Missouri. They chose to follow the northernmost branch, which they named the Jefferson after the president, because Sacajawea said it led to her country. The captains wanted to meet her friends, for they needed new supplies and horses to help them across the Rocky Mountains that loomed ahead across their path. But for days they saw not a single Indian.

Fearing that the Indians were alarmed by the size of his party, Captain Lewis went ahead with only a small band. Thus he crossed the Continental Divide and started down the western slope of the Rocky Mountains without excitement, for he was more concerned with making contact with friendly Indians.

They captured two terrified Shoshone squaws and forced them to lead the party to their camp on the Salmon River. The Indians were hostile—for some reason Captain Lewis had not brought Sacajawea with him.

Then a band of braves rode back along Captain Lewis's trail and met the main body. Sacajawea and one of the braves greeted each other with great joy, for they were brother and sister.

From then on, the Indians did everything possible for the party. They lent horses and a guide, an old man the white men named Old Toby. For five days they marched north into the Bitterroot Valley, and for ten more days they went west through snowstorms and rain on a terrible trail—later named by the Indians Lolo Pass, the nearest the Indians could come to pronouncing Lewis. On September 20, 1805, they burst out of the pass into the pleasant valley of the Clearwater River. The Flathead Indians there treated them well.

From that point to the Pacific, it was literally downhill all the way. They got canoes from the Indians and ran the rapids of the Clearwater and the Columbia rivers. In mid-November 1805, they beached their canoes and gazed on the Pacific Ocean, the first Americans to cross the continent.

The river mouth there is seven miles wide. There was some argument about which shore was best for a camp. The captains put the question to a vote. Interestingly to us today, the Indian woman Sacajawea cast a vote equal in value to either of the captains—and so did the black servant, York.

On the long way home, the party split up several times, zigzagging to map as much territory as possible in the single trip. They had their first serious trouble with Indians when Captain Lewis had to kill two of eight Grosventre warriors who tried to steal their horses and supplies.

On September 23, 1806, the expedition reached St. Louis and received a tumultuous welcome from a nation that had abandoned hope of ever seeing them again.

Pike's "Peek"

SO EAGER was President Jefferson to find out what he had bought in the Louisiana Territory and its exact limits that he did not wait for Lewis and Clark to return before sending out other bands to explore the new region. William Dunbar, a famous scientist from Natchez, Mississippi, explored the Ouachita River and discovered the hot springs that are now a national park in Arkansas. They probably were not the first white men there, for almost certainly Hernando de Soto had visited the springs in the 16th century. Several other parties tried to penetrate the Southwest, but they met Spanish patrols and were turned back.

Jefferson decided then to probe the northern limits of his new territory. He hired a Lt. Zebulon Pike and sent him northward from St. Louis in the fall of 1805. The 26-year-old professional soldier traveled in a keelboat with 20 men. He was supposed to find the source of the Mississippi River—and incidentally to proclaim ownership of the land.

All along their way they met Scotch and English fur traders. They built a log camp for winter quarters near modern-day Little Falls, Minnesota.

Leaving behind most of his men, Pike went on with two companions, carrying their supplies on sleds. They suffered great hardship in the hard northern winter, but every time they were about to collapse, they stumbled into a comfortable British trading post, where they were entertained. Pike was astonished at the luxury of those posts.

Not forgetting his duty, however, he ordered the traders to haul down the British flag and display the American flag. He forced the Indians to trade their British flags and medals for American emblems. The traders agreed amiably enough, for they knew that the minute Pike's back was turned they could go back to their old ways. Many of the Indians did side with the British in the War of 1812, just seven years after Pike's visit supposedly made them American citizens.

Pike returned to St. Louis in April 1806 with wonderful stories of his achievements and discoveries. He identified the source of the Mississippi River as Leech Lake—about 25 miles from the real source and about par for this explorer, who usually missed his goals by at least that wide a margin. (The true source at Lake Itasca was discovered in 1832 by Henry Schoolcraft. After several fruitless searches by army expeditions, Schoolcraft had the brilliantly simple idea of asking the local Indians where the river began. They led him straight to it.)

Pike's high opinion of his own record in the north won him another job, this time to explore the new territory as far as the Spanish border to the southwest. His true mission may never be known, for he was taking orders from Gen. James Wilkinson, one of the most villainous traitors in American history. The United States and Spain were hovering on the edge of war over the boundaries between Mexico and the Louisiana Territory. General Wilkinson was the supreme head of the American forces, charged with enforcing the American point of view.

And yet, years after the deaths of Jefferson, Wilkinson, and Pike, papers found in the secret files of the Spanish kings showed without question that the general had not only been a paid Spanish secret agent—Secret Agent Number 13, indeed—he had even signed an oath of loyalty to his country's enemy.

So crooked was General Wilkinson, however, that he was quite capable of double crossing the Spanish for the benefit of some dubious private scheme. Nobody knows, therefore, if Lieutenant Pike was sent on an honest exploration mission or on a spying job.

In any case, Pike left St. Louis on July 15, 1806, headed for the source of the Arkansas River, wherever that might be. (He left two months before Lewis and Clark returned to St. Louis from their triumphant and unblemished journey.)

Lieutenant Pike's incredible bumbling as an explorer began with his outfit. Even after the terrible sufferings of the previous winter in Minnesota, Pike set out on the Great Plains in late summer, knowing he would have to pass a winter on that almost subarctic prairie. His men were dressed in cotton overalls; his supplies included absolutely no winter gear.

Unknown to Pike, secret agents had sent word to Santa Fe of his intended trip. (Sending word to distant Santa Fe could have been done only overland, so clearly others had regularly used the trails Pike was supposedly going to explore.)

The Spaniards had outfitted a magnificent cavalcade of 600 soldiers, all mounted on spotless white horses. The two officers rode spotless black horses. They swept across the plains, warning the Indians to have no dealings with the Americans on pain of punishment. The Indians were impressed.

When Pike reached the Pawnee villages, his ragged little band of foot soldiers looked puny compared to the brilliant Spanish cavalry force that had just left. The Pawnees turned ugly. And the Pawnees were among the most ferocious warriors of the Plains Indians.

Pike ordered his soldiers to load their weapons and get ready to shoot their way out of the Pawnee village or at least to take as many Indians with them as they could if they had to die. Pike thought his men, with rifle, saber, and bayonet, could make the Pawnees pay a high price for victory.

"I believe it would have cost the Pawnees at least 100 men to have wiped us out."

The 22 white men and 3 Osage Indians of the party marched boldly through the camp and bluffed at least 400 Pawnee warriors.

On October 18, 1806, they came to the banks of the Arkansas River. There General Wilkinson's son took half the party and headed downstream with the hope of exploring all the way to the river's mouth—the same spot where Tonti had built a fort and near where Joliet and Marquette had turned back and De Soto had died. The other half turned upstream with Lieutenant Pike, supposedly in search of the river's source.

On November 15, 1806, Pike saw a tremendous mountain far to the west. It was his first view of what he called Grand Peak and what we know as Pikes Peak.

Near the end of November, they reached the point where the Arkansas broke up into several small streams. They cut cottonwood logs and made a fort for a winter camp, near modern-day Pueblo, Colorado.

Pike tried to climb Pikes Peak and failed, partly because the miserably thin cotton overalls he wore gave no protection from the cold. His whole party learned to make buffalo-skin boots with the fur left on, and they lined their cotton clothes with furs.

During their short side trips that winter, Pike came to the Royal Gorge of Colorado, within 35 miles of the source of the Arkansas, but with typical Pike bumbleship he called it the source of the Red River.

On January 14, 1807, Pike took a party of 12 soldiers and a doctor across the Sangre de Cristo Mountains into the valley of the Rio Grande. They left behind two soldiers with feet so badly frozen they could not walk.

That move across the mountains was serious. Pike *had* to know he was entering territory accepted as unquestionably Spanish by even the most pro-American geographer. Taking a band of armed soldiers into a foreign country on the verge of war is madness—or the act of a spy who wants to get a good look about under cover of being too stupid to know where he is. He crossed the Rio Grande and called it the Red River, even though the Rio Grande there runs north and south and the Red River runs east and west, as he knew. He built a fine fort on a side stream called the Rio Conejo and sat down to wait.

As he expected, the Spanish sent a force that arrested him and escorted him to Santa Fe. The governor there passed him along to the

73

OVERLEAF: *Zebulon Pike Entering Santa Fe*
By Frederic Remington
COURTESY OF REMINGTON ART MUSEUM,
OGDENSBURG, NEW YORK

authorities in Old Mexico. He was questioned and passed along, gradually eastward and northward. Though he was always under military escort as a prisoner, his men were allowed to keep their weapons. He was treated as an honored guest and entertained at many parties. He might not have been so welcome if the Spaniards had known that his men carried in their rifles little rolls of notes and maps covering the countryside he was crossing. A single pull of the trigger and the spy papers would be blown out of the guns as dust.

He returned to the United States on June 29, 1807.

Zebulon Pike is sometimes credited with pioneering the Santa Fe Trail that later carried thousands of tons of trade goods across the prairies from Missouri to Santa Fe.

He did no such thing, of course, for many French traders and a few Americans had long known every bend of the trail. Even the great mountain he supposedly discovered had been well known to Plains traders and to the Spanish for generations.

Zebulon Pike's story is a strange mixture of patriotism and suspected treason, of staggering incompetence and manly courage, of braggadocio and modesty. But it does make a good story.

The War of 1812 interrupted further army exploration of the west. In 1820 Maj. Stephen H. Long led a party into the plains from a fort where Council Bluffs, Iowa, now stands. They mounted the Platte River and the South Platte. One man of the party, incidentally, took the time to climb Pikes Peak, possibly the first man, white or red, to climb it.

Major Long returned to Fort Smith, Arkansas, in September 1820. He had discovered little that was not already well known, but he did leave his unfortunate mark on later history.

Despite the sea of grass he had crossed with its immense herds of buffalo, antelope, and wild horses, despite the teeming wildlife of the prairies, Major Long gave the Great Plains the name of the Great American Desert, a name that continued to appear on maps for 50 years.

"It is almost wholly unfit for cultivation, and of course uninhabitable by a people depending upon agriculture for their subsistence."

Major Long was talking about the present states of Nebraska, eastern Colorado, the Texas Panhandle, and Oklahoma. That very region today is one of the richest agricultural zones of the North American "breadbasket."

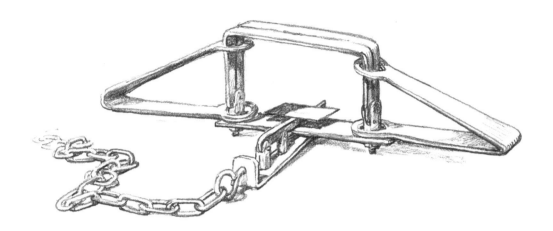

The Mountain Men

LEWIS AND CLARK, Zebulon Pike, Stephen Long, and above all, a host of nameless traders and *voyageurs* had made the plains known to the world. On the Pacific Coast, the Spanish had pushed up from Mexico, building a chain of missions and forts to meet the Russians pressing south from Alaska. The British had cut across the Rockies to the Pacific Coast at Vancouver. Outside of the Arctic, only one blank remained on the map of North America—the deep Rocky Mountains.

That last unexplored region fell before as brave and hardy a band of men as ever lived—the Mountain Men.

Even as Lewis and Clark were trudging home, two of their party—John Colter and Charbonneau, the husband of Sacajawea—refused to go farther than Fort Mandan. They turned down the joys of the triumphal homecoming ahead for the party in St. Louis to return to the mountains for a lifetime of trapping.

No sooner had Lewis and Clark made their report in St. Louis than a swarm of fur trappers and traders pushed up the Missouri, headed for the new lands the explorers told of, the mountain valleys thick with beaver.

They ran into a bad obstacle. The two Indians killed by Captain Lewis were Grosventres, close relatives of the Blackfoot tribe. The Blackfoot ruled the valleys of the central Rockies, and they swore eternal hatred for all white men. The Canadians farther north solved the problem by working only in large gangs powerful enough to scare off Indian bands. But trapping in large gangs is inefficient.

In the American Rockies, the trappers liked to work in small groups —usually no more than three or four at most and often only a single man and his Indian squaw. They simply took their chances, and many of them lost their bet.

For instance, the same John Colter who had crossed the country with Lewis and Clark was trapping with John Potts, yet another veteran of the Lewis and Clark march. The Blackfoot attacked, killing Potts. They lashed Colter to a post and were about to begin the tortures that preceded burning him at the stake. Colter called for the chief in the Blackfoot language.

"I have been a brave for the great captains Lewis and Clark," he said, "so I have a right to a fair fight with your warriors instead of a slave's death."

The chief had him cut loose and stripped naked. The Indians gave him a 300-yard head start and told him to run for his life. The best runners among the Blackfoot started after him. They had given him a start, but they wore moccasins, and he was barefoot. Within a few hundred yards, his feet were riddled with cactus spines and cut and bleeding from the rocks. But with his life at stake, Colter ran like a deer.

Colter shook off all but one warrior, who steadily gained on him. Just as he was about to feel the jab of the Indian's lance between his shoulder blades, Colter stopped suddenly and ducked. Surprised, the Indian tumbled head over heels over the crouching Colter. The trapper grabbed the Indian's lance, ran him through the body, and ran on.

At the Jefferson River, he dived in and swam to a logjam, where he hid while the Indians searched the riverbank.

Seven days later, naked and bleeding, Colter crawled on hands and knees into a fort 300 miles away, after completing a trip that would have exhausted a healthy man wearing warm clothing and carrying a good supply of food and water.

Colter later discovered the valley of geysers and smoking fumaroles we know as Yellowstone National Park.

Business was slow at some of the Rocky Mountain forts because the Indians worked only in summer and went down to the Great Plains in winter. So a Gen. William Ashley invented a new system that worked beautifully for 15 years.

Ashley formed a fur trading company in St. Louis and hired 90 white trappers to winter in the mountains. Each summer he sent a pack train to the mountain fort with supplies and trade goods. In midsummer the trappers came down out of the mountains for the "rendezvous," a kind of fair where they traded their winter's catch for enough supplies to carry them through another year.

At those rendezvous, mingled Indians and their squaws, a hundred or more trappers, Spanish traders from Santa Fe. For days they drank and danced, sang and whooped. They had shooting matches, footraces, wrestling. Sometimes high spirits would turn ugly, and a shooting or stabbing would carry off one of the trappers.

Among the Ashley men was Mike Fink, the legendary keelboatman who accidentally killed his best friend in a drunken shooting match. His unlucky shot made his name a synonym for treachery, and it remains so today.

Also an Ashley man was Jim Beckwourth, the son of a black slave and a southern planter. When his band of trappers reached Crow Indian country, as a joke they told the Crow chief that Beckwourth had dark skin because he was really a Crow Indian who had been kidnapped as a baby. To their astonishment, the Crow chief said he recognized the man as his own long-lost son. Jim turned the joke on his tormentors and joined the Crows, eventually becoming a chief.

"I told myself I can trap in their streams unmolested."

The black Beckwourth led the Crows in a war against the Blackfoot and completely wiped out one Blackfoot party. The Blackfoot, ironically, found out that a trapper had been with the Crows and redoubled their hatred—of *white* men!

By 1825, beaver in the far eastern Rocky Mountain valleys had become scarce, and the trappers had pushed west almost to the basin of Great Salt Lake. First of the expeditions to go from the Salt Lake basin to the Pacific left in the summer of 1826. The leader was Jedediah Smith, a mountain man. Smith became the most famous of all the guides who blazed trails for the flood of pioneers soon to cross the mountains for the rich lands beyond.

Unlike most of the rude men of the beaver valleys, Jedediah was well educated and highly religious. He had come to the mountains with the first batch of Ashley's men—a greenhorn in the trapping trade and a misfit among the jailbirds and toughs that Ashley had recruited. But he was a natural in his new craft and almost immediately became one of Ashley's chief lieutenants.

One of his comrades, no better than Captain Clark at spelling, gave an account of Smith's encounter with a grizzly bear.

"... he and the bear met face to face Grissly did not hesitate a moment but sprung on the capt taking him by the head."

Jedediah plunged a butcher knife into the bear's side, snapping off the blade and breaking the bear's ribs. With the bear run off, the party turned their attention to the leader's head. The bear had taken Smith's entire head into its mouth, tearing loose the scalp from the left eye on one side and the right ear on the other to the crown of his head. His right ear hung by a thread of flesh.

They threaded an ordinary needle and cut all the hair away from his scalp. Smith's comrade stitched away with his coarse cotton thread and got the scalp sewed back in place. He told the captain he could do nothing for the severed ear, but the captain said he must try.

"I put in my needle stiching it through and through and over and over laying the lacerated parts together as nice as I could with my hands."

Smith mounted his horse without help, and they made a camp beside a spring a mile away. The comrade summed up the day's work.

"This gave us a lisson the character of the grissly Baare which we did not forget."

While working the untrapped streams at the headwaters of a tributary of the Colorado River, Smith climbed a ridge and became the first white man to look out across Great Salt Lake.

The dream of sending furs from the interior down a westward flowing river to a Pacific port for transfer to China died hard. That Rocky Mountain stream flowing toward a Pacific port was all that was left of the Northwest Passage obsession, but it prompted Jedediah Smith and 17 companions to leave Salt Lake on August 26, 1826, searching for a stream that would lead to the California coast.

Their route led through present-day Brigham, Ogden, Salt Lake City, Provo, Spanish Fork, Payson, and Nephi. They followed the Sevier River to its source in the mountains, crossed the Continental Divide, and started down the Pacific drainage side on the Virgin River. When the Virgin River plunged into deep gorges, they struck westward across the barren desert.

The desert offered little game and no water. Smith and his men ate their horses, but the dried-out flesh had little nourishment. They were saved by reaching the Colorado River, which they followed downstream to the green gardens of the Mohave Indians, where they rested for two weeks.

From there to the California coast, the trail was easy to follow, for Indians had stamped it out for centuries, but it was across a dangerous desert.

On November 27, 1826, they reached the Spanish mission of San Gabriel, where the monks took them in and feasted them on corn and tender young beef.

Nobody on the spot realized it, but Jedediah Smith had just completed the Wilderness Road across a continent, the same road begun 51 years before when Daniel Boone and his axmen carved a highway out of the forest through Cumberland Gap, 2,000 miles to the east. That road through the grim Rocky Mountains and the southwestern deserts would

OVERLEAF: *Jedediah Smith*
By Frederic Remington
COLLECTION OF DR. HAROLD MC CRACKEN

soon funnel a torrent of American settlers into the southern California paradise, overwhelming the gentle Franciscan friars and their Indian wards, burying the Spanish culture under a flood of rude but virile American farmers.

The Mexican governor of California forbade further exploration, but Smith knew that the governor's authority stopped where the wilderness began—and Smith wanted the beaver in the mountain valleys that had never known the tread of a trapper. So he and his party went north through the San Joaquin and Sacramento valleys.

In the spring of the next year, though the snow in the High Sierras was still four to eight feet deep in the passes, Smith and two comrades crossed the range and descended onto the Nevada plain. The crossing had been so rough that it had killed two horses and a mule.

Crossing the cruel Nevada desert, headed for Salt Lake, they buried themselves in the daytime to escape the sun. As their horses died, the men ate them. Finally, one of the trappers stretched himself in the thin shade of a desert bush and told his comrades to go on without him; he preferred to die in peace. But just a few miles farther, they found a spring and went back after their friend.

On June 27, they saw the Great Salt Lake gleaming in the distance. Six days later, the three explorers, looking like skeletons, staggered into camp. The trappers there, who had given up Jedediah and his companions, fired a small cannon to salute his return from the dead.

Within ten days, Smith organized another party to follow the same grim path to California. Incredibly, one of them was a blacksmith who had just returned from the terrible desert crossing. Like the first party, they stopped to rest at the Mohave Indian village.

This time, however, the Indians first pretended friendship and then sprang on the party with war clubs, massacring 10 of the 19 explorers, including the blacksmith. Smith had only five rifles and little ammunition, so he gave the rifles to his best shots. He made a rude fort out of cottonwood logs. His men lashed skinning knives to cottonwood poles to make lances. They settled down to await the final attack.

When the Indians approached, three of the sharpshooters tried a volley at desperately long range. Each shot hit, killing two of the Indians and badly wounding a third. The Indians fled. The party was saved.

For nine days they crossed the California desert, hiding from the sun all day and traveling at night, chewing cactus stems for a drop of moisture. Once on the green Pacific slope, they turned northward and rejoined the trappers they had left behind the year before.

While Smith and two companions were off on a canoe trip, searching for an easier way back home through the Sierra Nevada than his last route, Indians fell on the camp and massacred all the trappers, except one giant who escaped into the woods by sheer brute muscle in throwing Indians out of his way. Separately, Smith's party and the lone trapper made their way northward to the Hudson's Bay post at Vancouver, across 750 miles of trackless wilderness peopled by hostile Indians. Incredibly, all four arrived safely, within two days of each other.

The Hudson's Bay Company, though keen rivals of Smith's trappers, organized a huge posse and rode down into California to punish the Indians and recover the loot. Smith never forgot the kindness of his Hudson's Bay rivals and never again poached on their territory.

Smith and a single companion rode back across the mountains to rejoin his comrades at the rendezvous. He went down to St. Louis loaded with a fortune in furs and tried to retire. But he could not.

He volunteered to lead a wagon train to Santa Fe. While scouting ahead of the train, he knelt down to drink from the Cimarron River. A band of Comanches surrounded him. Nobody knows what happened next, but two Comanches died before they brought down the greatest mountain man, and perhaps the greatest explorer, of all time.

The stories of the west are full of the names of the mountain great—Jim Bridger, Tom Fitzpatrick, Jim Beckwourth—but their adventures merely duplicate those of the greatest of them all. By 1840, the beaver had been trapped out, and the day of the mountain man was over. But by then they had penetrated the secrets of the Rocky Mountains and had thrown open the road west for the flood of settlers that would follow the discovery of gold in California in 1848.

A Continent Conquered

IN 1826, *The Missouri Intelligencer*, a newspaper in Franklin, Missouri, carried an advertisement:

> I WILL PAY 1¢ FOR THE RETURN OF THE APPRENTICE
> KIT CARSON, WHO RAN AWAY FROM MY HARNESS SHOP IN FRANKLIN,
> MO. HE IS 16, SMALL FOR HIS AGE, AND HAS LIGHT HAIR.

Thus began the career of by far the most famous mountain man of the Far West, the tiny but redoubtable Kit Carson. The contemptuous offer of a penny reward for his return may have measured his value as a teen-age flunky, but the undersized runaway had the stuff to make him a giant among the mountain men. At Santa Fe and Taos in what was then Mexico and is now the state of New Mexico, Christopher "Kit" Carson served a new apprenticeship more to his taste than the dull life back in Missouri. He willingly did the drudgery of packing bales of furs and cooking for trapping parties because he hoped eventually to cross the line from home-base servant to front-line hunter.

While waiting his chance, he discovered he had a remarkable skill with languages; he learned Spanish and Apache (which automatically gave him some grasp of the related Navaho language). He also picked up several of the Pueblo Indian tongues while steadily adding a smattering of mountain Indian languages.

He discovered another knack at least as valuable to a potential mountain trapper. Kit Carson was one of the best marksmen the nation has ever known. With any firearm, he quickly became the crack shot of any company he was with. He spent most of his career as a trapper, not trapping, but hunting to keep the working trappers supplied with meat.

When he was 20 years old, he made his first trip with a trapping party into the Colorado mountains. During that year's expedition, he traveled across the Continental Divide, through Arizona, and into California. His reputation as a hunter got him a spot the next year with Tom Fitzpatrick, then at the height of his fame as a trapping company captain. Kit rambled the Rocky Mountains summer and winter, steadily adding to his knowledge of the moutain passes and the Indian languages.

During those early years in the mountains, Kit fought a duel that lifted him to top rank among the mountain men.

Only five feet four inches tall, Kit Carson was dwarfed by many of the giants he worked with. Among them was a bully named Captain Ben, a hunter almost as good a shot as Kit but twice his size and strength. Captain Ben was widely disliked for his brutal manners, but nobody had dared to challenge him till he wore out Kit Carson's patience with his boasting before a frightened throng at a fur rendezvous. Kit challenged him to a fight.

Accounts of that fight differ wildly, and we may never know the truth of what happened—except that burly Captain Ben was soundly thrashed by the tiny mountain man and driven from the region forever.

Kit married an Arapaho girl and set up housekeeping at Bent's Fort, a major trading post on the Santa Fe Trail near present-day La Junta, Colorado. There, Mrs. Carson bore a daughter. The Indian mother died in childbirth. Kit accepted a job as hunter for a wagon train to St. Louis so he could take his baby girl to live with his brother and sister-in-law in the comforts of civilization. The Indians never forgot that Kit Carson had once married an Indian woman and was the father of a beloved half-Indian girl.

Meanwhile, farther north in the territory between the upper Mississippi and upper Missouri rivers—the same lands that had once been roamed by French Canadian *voyageurs*—an American of French descent named John Charles Frémont was acting as official surveyor for another Frenchman exploring the territory under contract to the U.S. Army. (The Frenchman was Jean Nicholas Nicollet but is not to be confused

with the Jean Nicolet who 200 years earlier had worn a gorgeous silken robe and carried two loaded pistols to a powwow with the Winnebago Indians at Green Bay in Wisconsin.)

Frémont was a first-rate mathematician, surveyor, and map maker. The Nicollet expedition was not really exploring, for the land had been crisscrossed by *voyageurs* for more than 100 years; this army expedition was plotting the region scientifically, so that travelers could depend on accurate maps rather than the accounts of trappers and traders who might not be overeager to help more people enter the territory.

Frémont did his work so well that President John Tyler, in 1842, asked him to go on another surveying expedition to map the South Pass through the Rocky Mountains in Wyoming, on the main route to newly opened Oregon country. To insure his company a steady supply of food, Frémont cast about for a hunter. At every turn, he heard about the great marksman Kit Carson. We aren't sure where they got together, possibly in St. Louis or possibly on a steamboat going up the Missouri River, but Kit agreed to take the job for $100 a month.

The pair must have been a strange sight among the great bearlike men who inhabited that frontier, for the tiny Kit Carson actually towered over Frémont, who was only five feet two inches tall.

The Frémont surveying party broke off work for the winter. By the following spring, the whole nation had become interested in the Northwest region where they were working, for the young United States and Britain were racing to see who would claim the Oregon country. Britain had a good claim based on the explorations of Alexander Mackenzie and the later voyages of Hudson's Bay Company trappers. The United States had a good claim based on the Lewis and Clark expeditions. Washington hoped that a competent survey and map of the region would strengthen the American claim.

Kit Carson guided the party from Great Salt Lake up the Bear River and northwest to the Snake River. Turning westward, he crossed the mountains to the Columbia River and followed it to the sea. When they reached that Pacific shore, they had accomplished their mission, but the pair decided not to go home without pushing into the unknown. So they recrossed the mountains, turned south, and explored the eastern slopes of the Sierra Nevada, a region unknown even to Kit Carson, though other mountain men could well have trapped that country for years. Things went so well that Frémont proposed the astonishing idea of crossing the Sierra Nevada into California, though winter was coming on.

Kit Carson had been in the Sacramento Valley on the other side of the mountains and knew that it was rich in game and that a fort at Sutter's Mill protected a small colony of Americans, though the area was Mexican. So, even with snow already six feet deep in the passes, he undertook to guide the crossing.

He showed the company how to make Indian-style snowshoes, and he ranged ahead hunting for game. The party suffered from the cold and hunger, and Kit Carson staved off mutiny only by assuring the men that he had just come back from the summit, where he had seen the Sacramento Valley in the distance. When Frémont's men emerged from the mountains, they became heroes of a national legend. The party returned home around the southern end of the Sierra Nevada.

In his report to Washington, Frémont was generous with praise for Kit Carson. Mrs. Frémont's account of her husband's voyages became a

89

OVERLEAF: *Carson's Men*
By Charles M. Russell
THOMAS GILCREASE INSTITUTE
OF AMERICAN HISTORY AND ART

national best seller, and Kit Carson joined Daniel Boone as a great folk hero, the ideal frontiersman.

In 1845, Carson and Frémont again marched toward California, this time by the desert route straight west from Great Salt Lake, about as grim a march as the West affords. While the map makers worked, Carson rode the countryside making discoveries. The region is peppered with reminders of his passage—Lower Carson Lake, Carson Lake, Carson River, Carson Sink, and, of course, the present-day town called Carson City.

Shortly after they arrived in California, war broke out with Mexico. Frémont apparently had secret orders from the president, who had expected the war before Frémont left for the West. Frémont helped take over San Francisco, Los Angeles, and San Diego.

Kit Carson, on his way to Washington with dispatches, met Gen. Stephen W. Kearny on his way to California with an army force, after having seized New Mexico without firing a shot. Carson turned over his dispatches to another officer and guided Kearny to California. Carson distinguished himself in the fighting there and later in the Civil War and the Indian wars that followed, but his exploring days were over.

Indeed, the day of exploration for anybody was almost over. After gold was discovered in California, tens of thousands of fortune hunters poured into the mountains and wiped out virtually all remaining pockets of unknown territory.

In 1869, John Wesley Powell, a one-armed veteran of the Civil War, led the last major exploring expedition in the United States down the Colorado River and through the rushing waters of the Grand Canyon. Frightened by the towering walls and roaring waters, two of his men deserted and were killed by Paiutes. Three days later, Powell emerged from the canyon at the junction with the Virgin River—near where Jedediah Smith had been ambushed by Mohave Indians. He was greeted by Mormon farmers and welcomed back to civilization.

In 1872, a party led by Almon Thompson left Kanab, Utah, and crossed the Aquarius Plateau. He found a new river and named it the Escalante after a Spanish priest who had explored Colorado. He found a new range of mountains and named it the Henry. Those were the last river and the last mountains discovered in the United States.

The Age of Explorers had ended in North America, south of the Arctic.

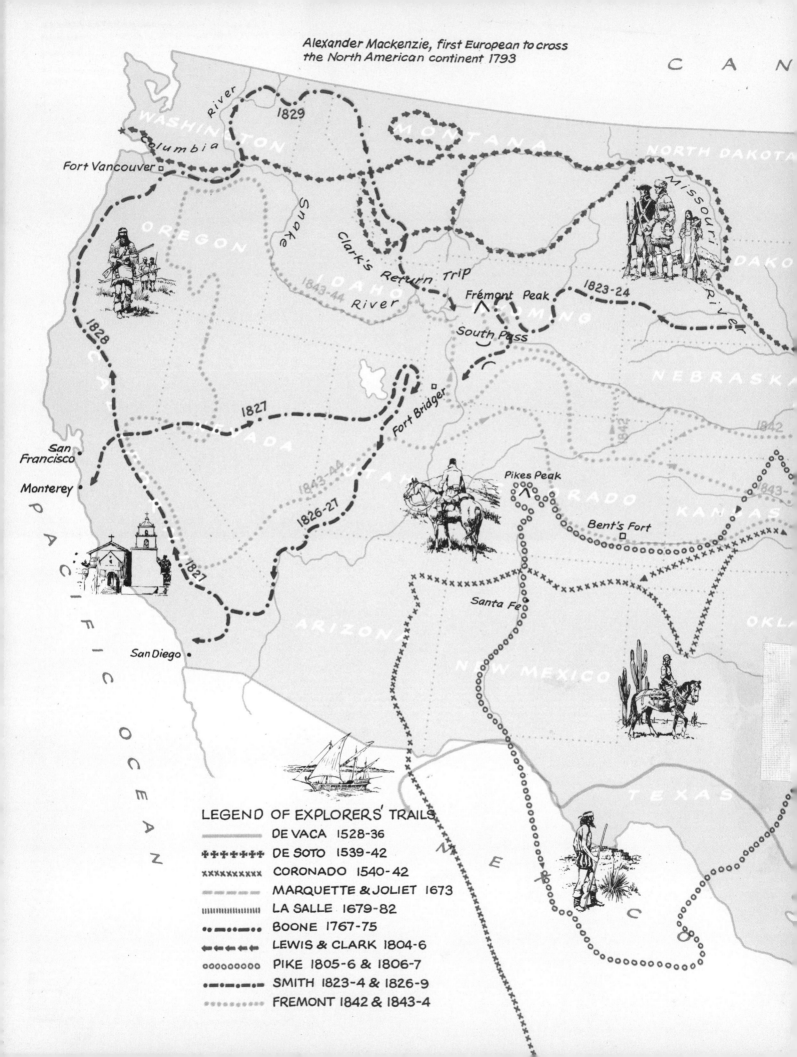

Alexander Mackenzie, first European to cross
the North American continent 1793

1829

Columbia River

Fort Vancouver

WASHINGTON

CANADA

MONTANA

NORTH DAKOTA

Missouri River

DAKOTA

OREGON

Snake River

Clark's Return Trip

IDAHO
1843-44
River

Frémont Peak

South Pass

WYOMING

1823-24

NEBRASKA

1828

CALIFORNIA

San Francisco

Monterey

1827

NEVADA

1843-44

Fort Bridger

1826-27

UTAH

Pikes Peak

COLORADO

Bent's Fort

KANSAS

1842

1842

1843-

San Diego

1827

PACIFIC OCEAN

ARIZONA

Santa Fe

NEW MEXICO

OKLA

TEXAS

MEXICO

LEGEND OF EXPLORERS' TRAILS

————————— DE VACA 1528-36
+++++++ DE SOTO 1539-42
xxxxxxxxxx CORONADO 1540-42
— — — — MARQUETTE & JOLIET 1673
ınıнıнıнı LA SALLE 1679-82
•—••—••—•• BOONE 1767-75
←—←—←—← LEWIS & CLARK 1804-6
ooooooooo PIKE 1805-6 & 1806-7
•—•••—•••— SMITH 1823-4 & 1826-9
············ FREMONT 1842 & 1843-4